SOUL TALK

A JOURNEY WITHIN

John Mandala

Battle Press
SATELLITE BEACH, FLORIDA

SOUL TALK

A JOURNEY WITHIN

Battle Press books may be ordered through booksellers or by contacting:

Battle Press
steve@battlepress.media
919-218-4039

ISBN: 979-8-9862-6326-7 (Softcover)
ISBN: 979-8-9862-6327-4 (eBook)

CONTENTS

ABOUT THE AUTHOR.. 7

PREFACE 8

DREAMS... 9

A LOVING LIFE 10

INTRODUCTION 11

CHAPTER 1 KNOW THYSELF...................................... 20

CHAPTER 2 JOURNEY INWARD.................................. 38

CHAPTER 3 GOD THE PUNISHER? 48

CHAPTER 4 SOCIAL RESPONSIBILITY........................... 56

CHAPTER 5 LIFE LEARNING 75

CHAPTER 6 LOVE AND FORGIVENESS 91

CHAPTER 7 THE CREATOR... 107

CHAPTER 8 SOULSHIP 119

FOOTNOTES 127

BIBLIODEX 137

"Mandala's ability to weave personal experience with deep insight has sparked my imagination to attention, revealing the vitality of another dimension found in humankind's commonality and our wholeness in talking with God."

Rev. Dr. George (Bill) Webber, President *Emeritus,* New York Theological Seminary.

DEDICATION

TO

JOHN-MICHAEL & ANNA-MARIE
ALL MY LOVE

ACKNOWLEDGEMENTS

I thank God first and foremost for all blessings bestowed upon me, and to my Mom, Jeanette, and my sister Mandy, who have been my continual support. To Joyce and Harry without whose love and forgiveness I do not know where I would be today. I would also like to thank those special family members and friends who have continued to be a supportive network all these years. My soulmate Pat, friends Lynne, Adrienne, my family, Valerie, Madeline, Francis, and many others who have believed in me through this journey. Special thanks to all those who have read, corrected, offered technical support, and made suggestions to my writings, especially Hank, Marge, Matt, Lorraine, John V., Waynon H. Durkins, jr., "Doc", and "House", without whose help and encouragement this book would not be. Lastly, I thank an incredibly special man and friend, Franco whose inspiration as an author resulted in helping me to realize my potential.

To my brother Steve, and friend Ronnie who have passed on into the spiritual realm. Miss you.

The enclosed poem, "A Loving Life", is one of many written by my father many years ago and is a clear indication of the spiritual man he was. This poem sums up the contents of this book eloquently.

ABOUT THE AUTHOR

John E. Mandala, MPS., B.A. graduated from Marist College and has a bachelor's degree in Psychology, as well as a master's degree from New York Theological Seminary. Mr. Mandala is author of *Poet's Touch, Reflections, After Prison A Way To Succeed,* and co-author of *Home Wine Made Easy, Freedom's Price* and a contributing Editor of *Alethia* and *The Contributor.*

The author has been studying and experiencing the way God speaks with us for many years.

PREFACE

Rarely in life do we take the time to understand what or who is guiding our path. Some of us are forced to do so, because of events that happen in our lives. *Soul Talk* is the story of my own experience and belief of the Divine essence within. It is my hope that this book will help others find the path of spiritual awakening. After reading this book, if you have any inquiries regarding the contents or wish to share an experience that you or someone else may have had, I would be glad to hear from you.

It is my belief, that "that of God within me" has called me to share the contents of this book. I have attempted to write in simple understandable language my own personal experience. I do not claim to have any of the answers to life. I try and live a life seeking truth in a spiritual walk connected to God. May the words and experiences described in this book open the heart and mind of all to God's unending and unfathomable love. I am convinced that God speaks with me continually in His language and I am open to His guidance. I believe that many people I have met in my life are messenger angels sent by God. I am blessed. Having been forgiven much I am compelled by the Spirit of truth to share the blessings. This book has not been written with theological analysis in mind, but with the hope to inspire reflection on our relationship with the spiritual essence within, and as a description of the depth and breadth of the human soul. Languages of the soul are varied and unlimited in God's ability to speak with humankind. It is my hope that you will understand that listening and speaking with God is natural and necessary to find a life lived abundantly and one filled with meaning.

DREAMS

Awake or asleep,
we all have dreams,
Of future hopes,
and unknown scenes.

Never knowing,
while we sleep,
What's for real,
or what will keep.

So, we wonder,
and contemplate,
About our life,
when awake.

Yet only in dreams,
does man escape,
Through fantasy,
in sleep or wake.

John E. Mandala

A LOVING LIFE

Love conveys no other thought
Than that, which it implies,
while greed and lust are products of
Man's avarice and lies.

Because His precious life did ebb
Nailed, upon a cross,
Let's heed His wondrous legacy of love
And justify His Cause.

August J. Mandala

INTRODUCTION

SPIRITUAL REALITY

"Why does one write, if not to put one's pieces together. From the moment we enter school or church, education chops us into pieces; it teaches us to divorce soul from body and mind from heart. The fishermen of the Colombian coast must be learned doctors of ethics and morality, for they invented the word **sentipensante** *(feeling-thinking), to define language that speaks the truth."* [1]

The statement above is a simple yet profound message to guide us on our journey to understand the language of God.[2] (Soul Talk). This is an important directive concerning how truth is hidden from the wise and knowledgeable, but **not** from the babes of this world.[3]

Gandhi once said,

"I claim to be a passionate seeker after truth, which is but another name for God."

Soul Talk is varied and is the Source of truth. Soul talk includes, but is not limited to, thoughts, ideas, feelings[4], intuitiveness, creativity, experiences, and joy, prayer, fasting, crying, silence, meditation, love, patience, art, music, messenger angels,[5] and other ways that we have communication with[6] God, ourselves, and one another.

Soul Talk is a language we are not familiar with, have

forgotten how to understand, or never knew existed. God speaks with us and listens to us individually and collectively. It is a two-way street. Our Spirit understands the languages of the soul, but we need to be taught how to understand what the Spirit is saying. It is not our fault that we have forgotten how to speak and listen to spiritual languages. As a starting point we need to admit to ourselves that we can communicate with God. One of our biggest hurdles is to recognize and acknowledge the existence of the spiritual realm and that languages of the soul exist. The ears of the Spirit are our heart and mind working together. Everything we hear can be judged with our heart and mind listening in unison and based in love. This is soul talk at the simplest and most profound level.

Confucius said:

> *"Never believe anything you hear, even if it is said by me, unless it speaks to both your heart and mind."*

An example of soul talk can be found in parables shared with us by many men and women throughout the ages. They speak to our heart and mind. Parables are one of our greatest examples of languages of the soul.

> *"Every happening, great and small, is a parable whereby God speaks to us, and the art of life is to get the message."* [7]

These parables are based on love and compassion for one another. They allow us the ability to transcend the human condition of difference and see each human being on a spiritual level. That is why a discussion of Jesus is central to this book. It is not because of any religion. Jesus did not come to establish a religion. Jesus was concerned about the condition of humankind both physically and spiritually. Jesus taught through parables that the way of transformation was a call based on our behavior and on a birth of the spiritual essence within. Jesus' call was to transcend differences and understand the common thread of humanity. This is communication through the soul and the life of the Spirit. Spiritual recognition and awareness become the most important attachment we have. We die in a human sense to materiality, to be born again spiritually (Matt 19:21). Our lives take on a whole new perspective as a result of spiritual transformation. This is the teaching of Jesus, a religion of the soul.[8] This is why we must come together in spiritual unity, embracing that which is evil, and overcome evil with the unity of love (Romans 12:21). We would then recognize and respect each other's spiritual essence. Jesus had firsthand experience of oppression as a Jew in a dominant Roman society. Yet, he was able to overcome the circumstances by understanding spiritual communication with God. Jesus taught that people should live life without oppression, injustice, and fear. No matter what anybody has ever told us, we are of value as unique individual human beings. No matter what our color, race, religion, class, gender, or any other group that people try and label us with, we must come to know that we are children of the Divine. We are as worthy as any other individual to live an abundant life. We must think a new vision to overcome the negative outlook we have been taught.

This can be understood when we realize and believe in our soul that this life is lived in this moment. This is a moment of spiritual eternity. Yesterday is gone, and the future is imaginary, life on this physical plane is now, this moment, one breath away.[9]

Sometime last year a lifelong friend, Ronnie, passed on into the spiritual realm. As I tried to understand Ronnie's transition, I received an interesting remembrance card from

Ronnie's soulmate[10], Carolee. I was so impressed by the saying that I brought it with me to share among the Sunday morning Friends[11] worship group. Upon arrival, the chapel, which is used for Buddhist services, was empty except for Sister Liu, a Buddhist Nun and volunteer at Sing Sing Prison. I invited Sister Liu to our service but she declined, feeling as though she could use the time in other beneficial ways. Remembering the card I had with me and being inspired I shared it with Sister Liu. In response she made the comment about life being only a breath away. I had to think about what she said but accepted the statement as a truth. Since that time, and almost one year later as I was finishing this introduction, Sister Liu was present again one Sunday morning. I wanted to have permission to use her name and her story as an experience in my writings. What surprised me is the story behind the story. Sister Liu told me that on July 4, 1976 she was looking out over a beautiful lake and enjoying the sunny day. Then all of a sudden, a bee stung her. It so happens that Sister Liu is quite allergic to bee stings. As a result, Sister Liu was taken to the emergency room of the local hospital. By the time she arrived her heart had stopped beating. It would take the next three months for recovery. In that time Sister Liu would begin a journey into her soul trying to understand why she was here, and what purpose life had. This would eventually result in her becoming a Buddhist nun, as well as understanding that; "Life is only one breath away." Had I not asked Sister Liu for permission to use her name and experience I would never have known the complete story, nor would I have been able to share this amazing parable.

All things happen for a reason, which we rarely understand. But I believe that all life is being guided, as I am, by that which Is unseen, but awesome.

Oswald Chambers, a minister to the troops in Egypt during WW 1 said:

> *"Spiritual truth is learned by atmosphere, not intellectual reasoning. God's Spirit alters the atmosphere of our way of looking at things, and things begin to be possible which never were before... Getting into stride with God means nothing less than union with Himself."*

The following is the keepsake card I was sent by Ronnie's soulmate Carolee.

> *"Death is nothing at all it does not count. I have only slipped away into the next room. Nothing has happened, everything remains exactly as it was. I am I, and you are you. And the old life that we lived so fondly together is untouched unchanged. Whatever we were to each other that we still are. Call me by the old familiar name. Speak of me in the easy way which you always used, put no difference to your tone, wear no forced air of solemnity or sorrow. Laugh as we always laughed at the little jokes that we enjoyed together, play, smile, think of me. Enjoy each and every day for me. Let my name be ever the household word that it always was. Let it be spoken without an effort, without the ghost of a shadow upon it. Life means all that it ever meant. It is the same as it ever was. There is absolute and unbroken continuity, what is death but a negligible*

accident. Why should I be out of mind because I am out of sight? I am but waiting for you for an interval somewhere very near, just around the comer. All is well."

Since Ronnie's transition, Carolee and I have shared many thoughts and have been able to help each other in understanding this experience and the spiritual life just a little better. Although Ronnie and I shared this life for more than 45 years, our friendship now continues through Carolee.

As Pierre Teilhard de Chardin, a Jesuit once said,

> *"We are not human beings having a spiritual experience, we are spiritual beings having a human experience."*

The statement above is a realization that the spiritual realm hidden from the eye is the most important aspect of this life. Unfortunately, humankind's attachment and reliance on the materialistic world has masked anything that cannot be perceived other than by the physical. In *Love and Will,* by Rollo May, we are given an excellent view of man's understanding of himself from a psychological perspective. Yet, I am disappointed that so much of what we are seems to have been forgotten, that of spirit. May states:

> *"One of the values of living in a transitional age, an age of therapy, is that it forces upon us the opportunity to see more deeply into those qualities which constitute the human being as human."*

In contrast, for thousands of years Eastern cultures have told us about shamans, psychics, faith healers, sages, clairvoyants and others who by spiritual power do mighty things, but we still do not believe.[12] Religious history has given us a clear picture of the spiritual realm in mighty miracles. However, we are reluctant to believe the existence of the spiritual world because we have heard that spiritual realms (what we can't see (the occult)) depict negative connotations.

It is time to understand that the soul experience is real and that we must look to embrace that which cannot always be seen on the physical level. It is time for us to become spiritually born. We need to embrace a new view and alternative understanding of living our human experience. Once we come to terms with our spiritual essence, we will live life differently.

Today, because of such reliance on the material world and the lack of belief that the spiritual world exists, we see a deterioration of morals, ethics, respect, and justice. Most people are obsessed with riches, but instead find unhappiness and hopelessness. As the dominant class continues to exploit and propagate materialistic ideals, many in society, find themselves with their "backs to the wall," having lost all hope, faith, and belief in God.[13] It is time for us to acknowledge our spiritual essence and stand together in solidarity of spirit. Although it may seem like an impossible task, we only need to look at the suffering of the masses and see the soul connection between us for inspiration and courage to make things change.

This is clearly expressed by Gustavo Gutierrez, *On Job* and shows the magnitude of our task:

> *"Our task here is to find the words with which to talk about God in the midst of starvation of millions, the humiliation of races regarded as inferior, discrimination against women, especially women who are poor, systematic social injustice, a persistent high rate of infant mortality, those who simply "disappear" or are deprived of their freedom, the sufferings of peoples who are struggling for their right to live, the exiles and the refugees, terrorism of every kind, and the common graves of Ayacucho."*

If we continue to be silent in the face of injustice, although in the heart of our being, our soul, we know and allow the exploitation of the masses to go unchecked, then we are as guilty as the oppressors.[14] Each day we must bear the cross of righteousness and come to transcend that which we see, with a new vision guided by the Spirit within. We must recognize the solidarity of our commonality to free ourselves from the preaching of the hereafter and live in the here and now. Present day religiosity will not solve the condition of humankind until we are willing to rock the boat and stand up for those with "their back to the wall."[15] It is time to arm ourselves and form a spiritual army of solidarity working towards peace, justice and truth. We as a people embracing the spiritual life must become the Good Samaritans' of this physical existence every moment of our lives. We must unite and demand justice, truth, and equality for all people.[16] We must use the principles of spiritual love and overcome evil with good.

St. John of the Cross a mystic once said:

> *"Where there is no love, put love, and you will draw love out."*

When we see wrong, we must expose it. Then we can claim like Martin Luther King Jr. *"I have seen the Promised Land"*, and it will be right here amongst us. Then the Spirit of the Divine will emerge and we will all recognize our essence as Children of the Divine.

This book is a story about awareness of self and others. My own awareness of the realities of my soul and the masses of people who stand with "their back to the wall" has been a tremendous awakening. I feel as though the tribulations I have gone through are part of my calling. I believe that God speaks to me in His language all the time. I see life as riding the crest of a wave but knowing that the truth lies within, and that's where I am going. I hope this book will help others find the truth within themselves.

Note: Bible quotes are taken from various versions and chosen for simplicity of understanding. Quotes with an * indicate an unknown source, but are included in the Biblio-Dex.

CHAPTER 1
KNOW THYSELF

"Jesus' message focused on the urgency of a radical change in the inner attitude of the (Jewish) people. He recognized fully that out of the heart are the issues of life and that no external force, however great and overwhelming, can at long last destroy a people if it does not first win the victory of the spirit against them." [1]

This statement is a key to a life lived abundantly. For it deals with the inner condition of humankind, the soul. It matters not what enters the body through the mouth and then passes out; it is what we speak and how we behave that comes from our heart (Matt. 15:19). This is the gift of a spiritual life. We need to understand that which is within. Today more than ever we see people acting out their frustrations instead of being able to communicate. Jesus used parables to allow us to see everyday life. This is an important beginning on the road to understanding our spiritual self.

Jesus' mission was a call to spiritual discipleship. It was a radically new way of thinking about the relationship with God. Not to God.

"Relationship to the Spirit and not primarily to the religious beliefs and cultural convictions of the times." [2]

Living a spiritual life is quite different from the normal way of seeing things. Jesus challenged the "contemporary wisdom of the holiness doctrine" and humankind's adherence to institutional rules. His way of life transcended the human experience by showing that worldly thinking or action could not frustrate spiritual living. Be all you can be in the spiritual army. Be free in mind and heart and look to the spiritual birth of the Divine in you.

As Joseph F. Girzone expresses through his character in *Joshua.*

> *"God respects people's freedom; faith is a gift. People must believe freely...True religion comes from the heart. It is a deep relationship with God and should bring peace and joy and love to people, not fear, guilt, and meanness. And worship has meaning only when it is free, God is not honored by worship that is forced under threat of sin or penalty. Nor is God honored by subservient obedience to religious laws devoid of law, God is pleased only by free expression of the soul that truly loves Him. Anything less is counterfeit and serves only the short-term needs of religious institutions..."*

Institutions create rules, which try to control people's thinking and their lives. Religious institutions separate people instead of allowing them to see their connectedness. Our search to understand who we are may very well be the most important mission of humankind in modern times. Forget about the labels we are given. Humankind was made to live free and live a life of creative integrity. Every human being has the creative essence of God and is of value. The very act of procreation is our greatest creative act. No one can tell us that we are not endowed with the creative essence of God. Yet, how many of us were taught this simple lesson?

Therefore, and unfortunately, many times our search to understand ourselves and come to know who we are is sparked by a startling event happening to us personally or to significant others. Only recently in different areas of the world and here at home, we have heard of catastrophes which caused people to look beyond their differences to their common humanity, that of the soul. In Florida, Ohio. Colorado, Georgia, and California only after many people lost, loved ones to senseless violence or homes to natural disasters did people come together in fellowship. Many times, it takes the pain and suffering on the level of a catastrophic event to see our commonality. It is usually this kind of experience that forces us to ask questions of ourselves.[4] In my case it has been coming to prison for causing the death of two people during a crime of passion. This is a debt I will carry with me always. I wish it never happened. However, because of one person who lived a spiritual life and had the courage and love to forgive me for causing her sister's death, my life has been changed forever. About two weeks after I committed these crimes, as I sat in my cell in the county jail, the officer called my name for mail. As I took the letter, I was utterly shocked that the letter was from Joyce, the sister of the woman whose death I had caused. I was afraid to open the letter and could only imagine what the contents might be. I surmised that it contained a plethora of hate, even though I knew this woman to be a gentle and kind spirit on prior occasions when we had met. Finally, I had the courage to open the letter. What I found inside was a shock. As I read the letter my heart began to pound, and tears came to my eyes as this woman had the courage and the love to tell me that she was sorry for what happened and that she forgave me. How could this woman forgive the person who caused her sister's death? I read the letter repeatedly, still not believing its contents. She told me about how she had tried to visit me in the hospital where I was recovering from self-inflicted wounds as I had tried to take my own life after taking the lives of two human beings. She told me that the police would not let her in to see me, telling her that in a few weeks she would hate me. She told them they were wrong that God had forgiven her for many things in her life, and that she forgave me. This was the beginning of a new life for me, as a glimmer of hope was set in my mind. Maybe I could someday forgive myself. Joyce went on to say that God would forgive me if I only asked. My whole life started to be revealed before me. I could not get over what Joyce had said and how she thought. If she could forgive me then her telling me that God would forgive me seemed right. Once I came to this kind of belief then I realized that maybe I could forgive myself. Soon after receiving this letter, I wrote to Joyce. I was scared at first but the more we corresponded, the more I understood the faith that she had in God. The more I experienced, the more I began to understand that God is a loving God. So many things were happening in my life at that time I was overwhelmed. I remember one day going to Reverend Torres and telling him that when I said my prayers at night that many times I would fall asleep and not finish. I told him how upset that made me. He simply said, "Is there any better way to fall asleep John? Stop worrying about it, God is on your mind and you are at peace." Shortly thereafter Joyce sent me a Bible which I began to read each day. There was a hunger in me, not only to read the Bible, but to understand what Jesus was trying to say. As I expressed this to Reverend Torres he told me that people were praying for me, and that I had to have faith. Then one day early on a Saturday morning I was in my bed and somewhere between dozing and sleeping, I remember thinking that if I wanted to learn more about the teachings of Jesus I would need a study Bible or other books that would help me. Then all of a sudden, the officer opened my cell and told me to come out into the hall. This was very unusual, and I was quite apprehensive. When I reached the hallway, Reverend Torres was standing there with a package wrapped up in gift paper. He said to me that one of the people in his congregation wanted me to have what was inside. As I opened the package, I was amazed, inside was a study Bible. I had never had any conversation with this woman or Reverend Torres about needing a study Bible. Yet only moments before being called, this was exactly what I had been thinking. God knows what we need before we even ask. I now know for sure that none of this is coincidence. All God's plans have a reason if we are only aware of His talking with us. Reverend Torres was clearly a modem day apostle of Jesus. He did not allow religious teaching to confine the spirit of God within. Even when we do something that is not within God's will. God still loves us.

St. Francis de Sales, Bishop of Geneva once said:

> *"The measure of love, is to love without measure."*

Our connection to one another emphasizes the wholeness of humanity. We begin to see our neighbor as ourselves no matter what our race, religion, or culture. The Good Samaritan story is a prime example of seeing past the physical to the core of human existence (Luke 10:33).

Seattle, Chief of the Suquamish Indians, said:

> *"Humankind did not weave the web of life. We are but one strand within it. Whatever we do to the web we do to ourselves."*

Like a kernel of corn, until it is planted and breaks open,

the real essence of the life within is hidden. Yet as the seed dies a metamorphosis from one state to another takes place, such as the caterpillar to the butterfly. Just because we cannot see everything, does not mean it doesn't exist. Many times, when traumatic life encounters break us open, then we can see inside ourselves.[5] That is the teaching of Jesus. It may be the first time we speak to our own soul or admit that we are more than what appears in a physical sense. The Spirit within and beyond the human experience is real. But how many of us believe it? Take one moment and focus on all the times you have been unable to explain something that has happened to you. Then you will begin to appreciate the spiritual realm of existence. How many times have we heard people say after someone close to them dies that that person is not only watching over them but has helped them through the painful experience that life sometimes presents? Living life on the physical plane cannot answer the question of humankind's inner condition. We must deal with spiritual answers by looking within our spirit existence.

In this regard, Howard Thurman makes both a statement and asks a question on the same page of the preface of his book, *Jesus and the Disinherited*, which seems radically opposed or a nuance divinely expressed.

Thurman states:

"The significance of the religion of Jesus to people who stand with "their backs to the wall"[6] has always seemed to me to be crucial.

Why is it that **Christianity seems impotent** *to deal radically and therefore effectively, with the issues of discrimination and injustice on the basis of race, religion and national origin?"*

The statement and question has touched me deeply and caused me to question everything I was taught, searching within for the answers. As a result. I am under the opinion that the religion of Jesus is not Christianity. But, I would say it was the learning of soul consciousness. Living in the present sense reality of the world of spirit. Therefore, God is every religion. For God is Spirit. If we look at the root of the word religion we would understand it to mean that which "binds" together. Therefore, a religion of the soul would allow us to understand the common soul connection between all of humankind, that of Spirit. This is Jesus' teaching, to show humankind how to speak with God, know who they are, and be able to rise above the circumstances of oppression to live a better way of life. Therefore, the religion of the soul is common among all humankind. Christianity cannot deal with the issues of life because it is not able to see deeply within at the core of our being, to that which is common and unseen, that of the spiritual existence. Religion today is based on the very same principles of the holiness doctrine that Jesus despised. It is no wonder that Jesus said, "Beware of those who call themselves religious" (Matt 16:6).

I have faith that God has called me to share words which I believe could make others know their own soul without having to go through what I have gone through personally. If we listened to the teachings of the Masters, we would understand this. I had to learn the hard way.

> *"A smart man learns from the mistakes he has made; a wise man learns from the mistakes of others."*[7]

Unfortunately, institutions have brainwashed us to believe it cannot be that simple. They are wrong. If we only listened to the voice within, we would be able to embrace the problems of life, understanding the experiences as one of growth. If we could view life simply and in a spiritual frame of mind, then we would be able to overcome **evil with good, falsehood with truth, and hatred with love,** and our world would be a vastly different place.[8] We could then find peace within, and peace without would abound. If we realized that we could all communicate in languages of the soul with God and one another, it would shed light on our own condition.

Robert Ellsberg, in a recent book *All Saints*, comments about Gandhi:

> *"Gandhi found a confirmation of his own inclination to distinguish between the message of Jesus and the teachings and practice of the Christian church.* **Jesus, as Gandhi observed, called human beings not to a new religion, but a new life."**

This is a powerful statement from two men who knew the truth. When we think about what we have been taught, most people believe they can only find God in religion. Yet all we must do is re-connect to the spiritual self and understand God speaking through our soul. There we will find God.

Joseph F. Girzone's, *Joshua in the City* says it very simply, yet profoundly,

> *"Religious leaders have always felt that in some way they had a mandate from God to control people's lives, and even their thinking. When people don't obey, they are made to feel they are disobeying God, and resisting God's grace, and jeopardizing their salvation. That is not healthy. God never intended that human institutions should have such control over people's lives,* **God made people free, they are His children.***"*

This statement clearly expresses the burdens that

religious institutions lay on people's lives. We must free ourselves from the kind of thinking which burdens free expression of the Spirit. I am convinced that in writing this book, I am being led to share truth of my own failings and personal revelations for the help of others.

Mother Janet Stuart said:

> *"If one gives joy to others, one is doing God's work."*

Knowing the person I was for 35 years before coming to prison, it is no less a mystery that I could have caused two people to lose their lives and attempt to take my own. I understand the reasons today, but it is no less overwhelming. I am convinced that I may have gone through my whole life without knowing who I was, had this not happened. This does not make it any easier to live with. I am alive while two people are not. Believe me, I wish it never happened. Yet, only after understanding the spiritual essence within, was I able to explain to myself the tragic behavior I thought was impossible of me. Today I still consider it a miracle that Joyce, the victim's sister was able to forgive me. This was a major point of change in my life. Because of Joyce I was able to believe that God forgave me, and that I could forgive myself. I am convinced that God is not finished with me.

As I was preparing to be sentenced for the crimes I had committed, many people who knew me wrote supporting letters to the judge. My soulmate Pat whom I have known for the past 35 years, made a statement to the judge which, has helped me to see the person I knew I was, even though I caused such a tragedy. Sometimes we fail to see who we really are until we read about ourselves from someone else's perspective. Although I could not separate the behavior from the person I was, Pat was able to. Although I have shared my sorrow with the families, I will always carry this sorrow in my heart. Pat said it very clearly and I will always cherish her insight. Pat was able to view me as a person looking deeper than the surface to that which is within, the person she had known for a lifetime who seemed incapable of committing the crimes for which I was charged.

> *"Whatever happened the day of the tragic incident which changed so many lives there will never be an answer. My personal exposure to this incident has certainly opened my eyes to the effects of the pressures, which surround humankind. These incidents also happen to the "Good guys" not just who we believe must be the bad guy - an element we never know or never certainly call our friends... While there is a price to pay for what we do wrong, a man with a conscience will pay for his action the rest of his life. [John] has a unique way of relating to those around him and has the incredible insight to reach those in need of direction. I ask that you consider my thoughts."*

I am incredibly grateful for the friends and significant others who have continued to support me for all these years. I am amazed at the new friends that have come into my life even though I have been in prison. The fact that I am in prison means nothing, yet everything, as it originally forced me to deep reflection. I value my friendships with people on the inside and the outside. Their problems and accomplishments are important. I take the time to listen to what they have to say. I have slowed down my life to smell a rose or look at a beautiful sunset. I try to say something nice to someone each day. We all need to see the beauty of life and affirm others' value and uniqueness. When we praise others, we praise God. The following poem is an example of slowing down my life and looking at the creation expressed.

CLOUDS

RAINBOWS OF LIGHT
CLOUDS CREATE,
OF SUNBEAMS DANCING CROSS
HEAVEN'S GATE.

OF PRISON VIEWS
WHO'D EVER THINK,
OF SOULFUL NOURISHMENT
A HEALTHY DRINK.

OF DREAMS AND HOPES
BEYOND THE WALLS,
OF ENDLESS DAYS
AND FREDOMS CALL.

OF LONELY NIGHTS
AND BUSY DAYS,
OF FRIENDSHIPS MISSED
WHO KNOWS THE WAYS.

AND SO, THE CLOUDS
EXPRESS GOD'S FREELANCE FORMS,
WITHOUT WHOSE PRESENCE
WOULD BE EMPTY STORMS.

Many times, while speaking with friends on the phone, they will comment that so few people listen to what they have to say. We have become so caught up in worldly affairs that we rarely listen to other people, or praise people for their accomplishments. Time is the greatest, blessing we have, and we fail to recognize and appreciate it. If we only slowed our lives down and took the time to look at a sunset and admire the stars, our lives would be better. Likewise, if we take the time to tell someone we love them or show them we love them by doing something good for a person who has less than we do, life would be much more rewarding. When we see each other as spiritual beings, we begin to see the essence of God within.

Several months ago, one of the founding fathers of the Sing Sing Friends Worship Service announced his plans to be moving to another state. After the usual discussion that he would be missed, men and women in the group began to share their positive feelings about our Friend Norman Goerlich while he was present. So often we wait until someone dies and then discuss how good a person they were. What a pleasing experience to talk about someone in a positive light when he is present so he can understand how much he is loved in the here and now. This is a lesson we should try and learn. To say something good about people while they are here. Something simple such as "have a nice day" or "you look nice today" can make all the difference in a person's life.[9]

In prison I have come to know some of the very subtle changes that happen to a person. Communication between prisoners concerning personal feelings, problems, hopes, dreams, disappointments, and relationships are rarely more than superficial. Prisoners build walls around themselves for protection. Very rarely do men share their lives with one another. As a result, some men look within themselves and engage in deep reflection and meditation. This I believe is the reason why so many men and women find spirituality about themselves they have never known before. Prayer and meditation or self-reflection begins to open the flow of spiritual knowledge and power from another plane of existence.

I am amazed not only at my own accomplishments but also those of many men and women in prison who find an essence they never knew they had. Men and women who create paintings, leather work, pottery,[10] writing, poetry, wood carving, card making, creative cooking,[11] teaching, patience, caring, and the list continues. How could this be? I believe it is knowing, sometimes for the first time in our lives, the creative spirituality we all possess as children of God.

My biggest problem was that I was a compactor. Feelings from 30 something years of my life were bottled up inside of me and was one of the reasons why I was in jail for the crimes I had committed. "Emotions are poor masters but good servants."[12]

However, there is a detrimental effect that occurs to people in prison, as the ability to communicate with others becomes more difficult. I think that is why Jesus stressed that people should visit men and women in prison. Jesus knew the soul experience of solitude, or perhaps he also knew the spiritual awakening that needed to be shared with others (Matt 25:36). This is the Spirit working through others. I am grateful that today I recognize and understand languages of the soul and messenger angels. Today as my spirituality continues to grow, I know who I am.

As prisoners our ability to communicate with volunteers and caring people is one of our most important freedoms. In this regard, a woman by the name of Elva[13] came to the jail as a volunteer each week and shared with us her spiritual walk and how God had moved in her life. As part of the Spiritual program, volunteers of Youth for Christ visited the jail to speak with troubled young men. Peter, the Director, and a personal friend of Elva heard that I had made great strides in understanding my spirituality as Elva had shared some stories about me with him. One day, as Peter was leaving the prison, he stopped me in the hall and asked me a puzzling question. "What do you have in common with Moses, David and Paul"? I replied. "I don't know." Peter then said, "You all caused the death of a person(s)." I was a little bit surprised by Peter's honesty and straightforwardness. Peter then said: "Do not lose hope. God forgave them and used them in a powerful way." A simple statement spoken so many years ago made me realize how God uses us. After almost 9 years in prison, I had the opportunity to meet with Peter again. I mentioned the statement he had made to me and that God had in fact used me powerfully. I was not prepared however for what Peter then said:

> *"Shortly before I met you John, one of the first troubled youths I was helping had been killed. I knew him since he was 10 years old. At eighteen he was killed. For a long time, I was unable to forgive the man that killed my friend, but after I met you and we spoke, and you told me of the forgiveness that you had received I was moved by the Spirit of God working through you. Eventually I was able to forgive the man who killed my friend. It was a cleansing experience, having carried the hate within my soul for so long."*

Even when we do not know. God is always working.[14]

To say the least I was surprised at Peter's comment and realized that God had been using me in ways I did not know.

For this reason, outside support groups are so important. The lack of human interaction affects the psyche in ways that few people realize. Only recently have health care professionals in the Social Services realized the difference between our Intelligence Quotient (IQ) and our Emotional Quotient (EQ). Our emotional growth is directly related to understanding who we are, children of the Divine.

In a recent article by Guru Dev, *Aging With Wisdom*[15] he makes the comment that:

> *"The true journey of life is to return to the Source" ...There are no answers to your life to be found outside of you. The answers lie within...Yoga and meditation are practices that develop our capacity to attune to our internal messages. As you move towards your inner Source, your internal knowing guides you to the next step in your life.*
>
> *You receive the higher calling of your spirit to live entire truths of love beauty', peace, service and full creative expression."*

Guru Dev's path to what he calls the Source with a capital S. clearly states that inner awareness is understood in languages of the soul. Although Guru Dev may dance to a different drum, it is his belief that knowing that of our soul within, is our highest attainment in life.

Dom Bede Griffiths, a monk and Sannyasi, once said:

> *"The call of the Church today is to transcend the limits of institutional structures and to open itself to the presence of the Spirit in the Church and in every Christian."*

We must change our attitudes and allow that of God to gird us up, and in faith, hope, and love, come together in God's strength. The power of evil is real in many ways. It is our calling to grasp the ideas of freedom and creative individuality and a greater unity of the soul through spiritual birth and make changes. Those of us who have been blessed with spiritual awareness must stand up to the injustice everywhere.[16]

In a Guidepost publication by Norman Vincent Peale titled *Source of Courage*, the statement is made:

> *"Often, people who act wisely in an emergency say it* **comes not from them, but from a mysterious source.***" Peale then says: "I* **think** *it was the power that God has planted deep in all of us. I think it was the* **plus factor."**

How strange to read a pamphlet written by a man who is read by millions of people and have it referred to his idea of God as the plus factor. Have we become so distant from God that we think it is God, instead of *knowing* that we are His children and His creation? Here is a man that millions of people read all the time and he calls this force the Plus Factor instead of affirming that of God within each one of us. No wonder it is so hard for us to understand God talking with us. Why do we find God working in our lives so incredible or mysterious? One reason is, we do not know who we are.

I remember and now recognize one of the first times while in prison that God spoke to me to share His word. I was having a conversation with a man nicknamed Blood. He was telling me about a white woman that was visiting him and trying to push religion on him. Then one day we were conversing and looking out a window up on the 4th floor of the jail. Blood made the comment that he did not believe anything that he could not hold in his hand. As I looked outside I saw a tree and its leaves blowing back and forth, I turned to Blood and asked him if he saw the leaves moving, he said, yes. I then said, well you can't see or hold the wind but those leaves are not moving by themselves. Blood looked at me and said. I can't talk to you anymore. From that moment on he never spoke with me again, even though I was in the cell right next to him. God had given me a truth to share. However, this man Blood did not want to accept the truth I had given him. I am not saying that this proved that there is a God, but it was a truth that could not be questioned. Languages of the soul are like the wind; they are personally experienced.

George Sand once said.

> *"We must accept truth even if it changes our point of view."*

The following poem resulted from that experience.

Whispering Wind

> *Listen to the wind*
> *As it whispers to your soul*
> *From where it begins*
> *No one really knows.*

It cannot be seen
With the human eye
Yet it blows the clouds
In an ever-changing sky.

Its message has been hidden
To most of the world
Like the old scriptures
Which were constantly unfurled.

So, let your heart be open
As you feel the force
The language of God
Is really the Source.

Today I am convinced that God was talking directly to me and continues to do so in His language. A language and a spiritual existence I had forgotten. Today listening with the ears of the spirit (heart & mind) I know God speaks to me all the time.

Only recently through a man I have met in the prison system have I come to understand who I am in a deeper way. For many years I did not realize why I did some of the things I do. I never knew that my *"Spiritual Identity'"* [17] was that of a weaver. Today I realize it is the spirit speaking to me.

In prison men must hide their feelings, otherwise they are considered soft and prey to people who take advantage of the so-called weak. For most of my life I never understood why I would cry when I saw an emotional movie. But, I know that it has nothing to do with being strong or weak, it is our personal connection to the essence of the Divine within. Even after being in prison all these years. I am glad that I can feel the spirit talking to me. This is soul talk in the simplest form.

CHAPTER 2
JOURNEY INWARD

About one year ago at Sing Sing Prison, and as part of the Friends Worship Meeting, I had the opportunity to meet Lama Surya Das, considered to be one of the most prominent American Buddhist monks. I was impressed by his sense of peace and considered him one of the few "Soft Souls[1]" I have met in my life.

In his new book, *Awakening the Buddha Within*, one of many books that appeared simultaneously and unexplainably to me, Lama Surya Das teaches the important aspect of communication with our inner being.

He states:

"Those of us who embark on spiritual paths are motivated in different ways. Some of us want to know the unknowable; others want to know themselves; still others want to know everything. Some people want transformation; others want miracles. Many want to alleviate suffering, help others, and leave the world a better place. Most of us are seeking love and fulfillment in one way or another. Everyone wants inner peace, acceptance, satisfaction, and happiness. We all want genuine remedies to feelings of despair, alienation, and hopelessness. Don't we all want to find spiritual nourishment and healing, renewal, and a greater sense of meaning? Don't we hope to find our true selves, all we are and can be? Is there no greater connection, no deeper purpose and sense of truly

belonging? Rejoice! You are living the core issues grappled with by every consciously alive human being. This is no small thing - this is 'Big Time,' the Great Way walked by all those who have awakened to freedom, peace, and enlightenment. You're in the heavyweight division, wrestling with multi-dimensional angels of life."

Surya Lama Das is saying that there is something within that needs to be awakened. The questions revealed to me are: What needs to be awakened? How long have we been asleep? How do we wake up that within which is asleep? There are many paths for us to journey upon, none of which are right or wrong for answering these questions. For me, the guide summarized below is a simple way of getting to know our inner being.

In a recent article in Friends Journal, March 1999, *Experimenting with Light,* Sue Glover[2] outlined the steps to awaken that of God within and hear Him speaking with us. Ms. Glover clearly stated that each of us has a unique and individual experience. We cannot give anybody the clear-cut roadmap, but we can share what does work with others, to understand a little better that of the spiritual essence within. The following six steps are only a guide that worked for others. I am extremely glad to see a simple expression of how we can follow this process. There is nothing special about it. I have added my own thoughts within this example. I would suggest that you find a quiet place at home to begin. Quiet is inside us all, but in the beginning noise around us can be distracting. Hopefully, you will also find the peace within, we all possess.

1. *Relax the Body and Mind - Be conscious of your thoughts and images and then let them go. Try to stop thinking about anything.*

2. *Without changing horses from your open state above - let the real concerns of your life or the people in your life emerge. As this comes to consciousness - without thinking about answers - ask questions such as - What is going on in my life? Do not try to answer the question but allow an answer to come. Try and be separated from this procedure intellectually. Remember God speaks in languages of the soul.*

3. *Now focus on one issue that emerges. And let it grow on its own until you see it in your mind's eye a vision of the whole. Try not to think but just let it exist.*

4. *Then ask yourself - Why is this an issue? Again, try not to think but gently continue to be at peace with the issue. Resist thinking of answers. If an answer emerges then -*

5. *Welcome and embrace it - even if it is confusing allow it to grow and if it is truth you will know. Submit to it and allow it to grow by itself.*

6. *Lastly, consider what is being said and how it will affect your life. Be open to its truth as it speaks to your life and soul, the Spirit within.*

If after you have gone through these simple steps you find a part of you that you have never known, enjoy that of God within speaking directly to you. Speak back to the voice within in thankfulness. Be at peace. Remember however, that the spiritual life is a blessing and once realizing that we have been blessed by awakening, we then realize that we are required to share truth as we continue our journey (Luke 12:48).

An example of this follows from an exceptionally good friend of mine Angel L. Rivera, a fellow graduate of the New York Theological Seminary[3] and a child of God. Angel is free, but none the less behind the walls of prison. He shared an article written for Voices of the Class of 1998.

The article titled *Releasing Our Human Dignity*, stated:

"When we discover our divinity, we immediately want to teach people how to free themselves from ignorance... Thus, we have an absolute obligation to inspire others to discover their great divinity within themselves."

As part of my prison Journey, I met a very special man. Rev. Dr. George W. (Bill) Webber, President Emeritus. New York Theological Seminary[4]. He taught me an incredibly special lesson some years ago. But I never quite understood what Bill was saying until recently. One of Bill's favorite Bible passages is Jeremiah 29:15 "*Seek the Shalom of the city.*" Wherever you are, try and do your best. Be open to the leading of the Spirit of God within you and try and walk worthy of the vocation that you are called to be. Most people would laugh when they hear something such as this from a man in prison. Yet prison can be a great learning experience. It is time we understand that being a Christian and being called to live as a follower of Jesus are different. Bill is a Jesus follower. This man's ministry in prison[4] is God sent and his effort led by God's Spirit is an example of dispelling the view that prisoners are different than us, are worthless. One of Bill's favorite statements, which I have come to cherish, is that

"We will not be judged by the purity of our actions, but by the integrity of our compromises."

I have shared this with you because as I am writing this book, God is leading me each day. As I talk with people and experience God speaking to me in His language, God is telling me to indict the people of this generation. It is people that cause war and punishment to come upon humankind, not God.

The following passage is an example of how God

continually speaks to me. On Wednesday evenings I am an inside volunteer in the Catholic Bible study. This past week I was speaking with visiting Volunteer seminarian, Ed Cipot, a spiritual man whose insight I have come to know and appreciate. Throughout the evening we discussed some of my ideas and his responses concerning this book. At the end of the evening, he suggested that I read a document from Vatican II. The below quote is from that writing and was very instructive in my thinking concerning God's love for all humankind. The more I read and research, the more the adage seems applicable to religious institutions. The institutional church fails to practice what they preach.

> *"The plan of salvation also includes those who acknowledge the Creator, in the first place amongst whom are the Muslems: These profess to hold the faith of Abraham. Nor is God remote from those who in shadows and images seek the unknown God, since he gives to all [humankind] life and breath and all things...Those who, through no fault of their own, do not know the gospel of Christ or His church but who nevertheless seek God with a sincere heart, and moved by grace, try in their actions to do His will as they know it through the dictates of their conscience - those too may achieve eternal salvation. Whatever good or truth is found amongst them is considered by the church to be a preparation for the Gospel and given by Him who enlightens all [humankind] that they may at length have life."*

Having read the above statement found In the *Dogmatic Constitution on the Church. Vatican II Lumen Gentium (Light of the World) November 21, 1964,* I was surprised to find the language so universal in comparison to being brought up in a religion which seemed so exclusive. The above writings talk to that of God within me and illustrate God's love for all humankind in their search for truth. Who are we to try and limit God? Yet this is what institutions seem to do all the time. No wonder institutional religion is dying a slow death, for it does not address the inward center of humankind, the soul and the living Spirit within. As prisoners our ability to communicate with volunteers is one of our most important freedoms. Prisons are built just as much to keep people inside, as they are to keep others out. One of the greatest blessings that men and women have in prison is from people in the community who really care about those who are in prison. My fellowship with people from Rye Presbyterian Church, Scarsdale Quakers, Purchase Quakers, Ossining Prison Ministry, Our Lady of Hope Catholic Church, Prison Fellowship, The Osborne Association. Rehabilitation through the Arts[5], and many more organizations who care about people is the soul fellowship that defies all differences.

These people really care, but the authority's lord it over their heads in such a way that they are scared to do anything that will jeopardize their volunteer status and ability to come into the prison. Recently a long-term volunteer was suspended because men were discussing their unhappiness about the illegal parole board practices as part of their worship service on social justice. An officer was listening and reported this discussion to the higher authorities. This is a social justice problem, which Jesus addressed. Yet the authorities believe they can orchestrate the way people worship their religion. This is real injustice.

Thomas Merton once said:

> *"The Christian life and especially the contemplative life is a continual discovery of Christ in new and unexpected places."*

I remember having a discussion with a man who was aghast that I did not know what was going on in the early 70's and therefore oblivious to the injustice, racism and downright separateness that pervades our society. In retrospect, I understand what he was saying, because I had never experienced or opened my eyes, mind, and heart to the suffering of those who were being treated differently than I. It would be easy for me to say that I was naive or that I just did not open my eyes to what was going on in other people's lives. It is difficult in life to see the plight of others when we are comfortable or misinformed.[6]

Realistically speaking, in white American educational institutions both injustice and racism are rarely exposed and spoken about in classrooms. It is a fact that when we have white Euro-centric authors writing about history they are going to write about those who are in power. Even today with the great leaps in knowledge and historical evidence, mainstream education does not share truth and explain the true history of those peoples of this earth who have discovered scientific facts and or startling developments. It is a shame that the history of many great people has been diluted because of indifference.

I recently watched a powerful movie by Toni Morrison, *Beloved* and was sick to see the treatment of black men and women by whites. No wonder we want to sweep this under the carpet. However, this only emphasizes my point that we must look beyond the physical and experience that of the Spirit, within. *There is neither Jew nor Greek, bond or free, male or female, for we are all connected through the soul.*

(Gal. 3:28) The spiritual essence of being one. This is a lesson we must learn and begin to embrace: otherwise, we are on the road to destruction. I am thoroughly ashamed to call myself an American when I see the horrible history of this country concerning Black people. This is part of American history, which I am only starting to know. Therefore, it is so important to rise above differences. This does not mean we can write history to reflect falseness. No wrong must be exposed for what it is. We must come to take responsibility for the future. The past is gone.

In his introduction to *On Job*, (*Suffering of the Innocent*), Gustavo Gutierrez gives a remarkable theological explanation of our relationship to God. Unfortunately, for most people, and even for a student of theological training, it takes several readings to understand what is being said. This is why the masses are lacking the ability to understand God talking with us. This is why explanations such as given in the book, *Joshua*[7] and here I hope, are helpful and I believe important. Plain language is needed in our understanding of God and of human history based on truth. Then we will begin to communicate with God and each other. This is why it is important to hear God speak to us in His language.

Upon reflection, the High School that I attended had a graduating class numbering over one thousand students, yet there were no Blacks or Hispanics in that school. Strangely though, I do remember in junior high school a brother and sister who were Chinese and were in my science class. The only reason I remember them is that we competed against each other for the highest grades in science. Yes of course they were different from me, but I never remember thinking to myself that they were inferior or not deserving of the respect that everyone else should receive. I never remember my mom or dad being or acting in a racist manner or being hateful against anybody or saying things that would make me look at people differently. But I do not remember them being concerned about others who were suffering either. It was when I was almost twenty years old and moved to Florida that for the first time in my life I would be exposed to racism. I see now how sheltered a life I lived. I am the first to admit that I have a lot to learn. Even being a prisoner, among prisoners, the stereotypical label of a white boy, honkey, or cracker does not overcome the hatred and lack of trust by men of color. I don't blame them for their feelings. Prison has brought home to me the pervasive racism experienced by those who are different. Being in prison has allowed me to see the shameful way people act towards one another. Only when we as human beings transcend the physical difference and begin to live in the Spirit will this world be a different experience.

After reading the insightful book *Black like Me* by John Griffin for the first time in my life I was able to understand a glimpse of the pervasive racism in this country. This man had the guts and the inner voice to try and understand what it was like to be a black man in America. I am personally horrified by what one race of people has done to another because oi the color of their skin. This continues today and is an indictment on all people including the so-called religious for allowing it to continue. Maybe Jesus believed in a utopian society that could look past the differences of humankind because of His Divinity, but can we? This is the test of humankind for our world today. To look at the heart of each individual and see that of God within. That of the Spiritual essence or divine being within. Spirit has no color, race, gender, age or identifying mark, other then what the Bible calls fruits of the Spirit, which signify a life of action lived righteously. I am convinced that we must take a new approach in our view of humankind, otherwise we are finished. This world cannot last much longer when because of difference we hold ourselves superior, as if others are inferior to us. We are all different in our physical appearance, yet who are we to judge one another as to our abilities because of our physical manifestation. We all carry within our being that of the Divine, therefore we are all connected. We must re-educate our citizens and be honest about the psychological warfare government has used against minorities to ensure their lack of self-esteem and ability to succeed. Our African American brothers and sisters were stripped of their cultural history and exploited in the name of capitalism. This wrong can only be corrected when we as a people know that our essence, is that of the Divine, and we transcend physical difference. Likewise, it is time every one of us takes responsibility for our actions today. We cannot blame people who are alive today for what happened in the past. We need to reconcile our past wrongs and look to redemption for all with a new vision for the future.

We must overcome what Thurman calls the "three hounds of hell that track the trail of the disinherited." These are fear, deception, and hate.[8] Thurman postulated that:

> *"We must abandon our fear of each other and fear only God. We must not indulge in any deception and dishonesty, even to save your lives. Your words must be yea-nea; anything else is evil. Hatred is destructive to hated and hater alike. Love your enemy that you may be children of your father who is in heaven."*

This is Jesus' religion. We must live the life of spirit while in the body. This is how we can overcome our fears. Therefore, the religion of the soul must be embraced.

CHAPTER 3
GOD THE PUNISHER?

As a young man growing up on Long Island with Sicilian heritage. I still remember suffering the taunts of others and being called a wop, grease ball, and a dirty Italian. So, I have a small glimpse of prejudice associated with being different. On the other hand, being raised as a Roman Catholic I was one of many who were like me. I clearly remember in my Father's room a Bible that sat on top of his big brown dresser. I never once remember it being taken down and opened or studied by anybody in our family. I am sure Mom would take it down to dust, but that was about it. The Bible was a once-a-week experience at church on Sunday. That does not mean we didn't say prayers at the dinner table or prayers at night when going to bed. In fact, one of the more pleasant memories of my childhood was the nightly ritual of Mom coming up to our rooms to say prayers and goodnight to her three children. Mom and Dad tried to live the Bible teaching, even though they didn't read it.

Being brought up in the suburbs in what could be considered a middle-class family life was pleasant. Sunday was a day of church going and then off to either grandpa's house or grandma's house for the family get together. I grew up in a love filled atmosphere. When my parents weren't working, they would attend church regularly with their children. At that time, the Mass was said in Latin so little of the Mass had meaning. The most remembered event of the Mass was the Eucharist, but there were so many do's and don'ts associated with that, that I would only partake of the Host at special times of the year to do my "Easter or Christmas duty" as it was said back then. Strangely, communion and Jesus saying that we should *"Do this in memory of Me"*[1] seemed to be important, but all the other rules were perplexing. Was Jesus talking about communion only or was he talking about the whole Last Supper experience? Jesus seemed to say that he loved everybody and was being a servant. But religious people were saying that God was a punishing God. I got to a point of not knowing what to believe.

Each day is a miracle, if by faith we see life as such. What a powerful lasting memento Jesus gave us in the Eucharist. Love God and love thy neighbor. Pretty simple stuff. Why is the miracle of the Passover so hard for us to believe? That story which has been passed down by Jewish tradition for thousands of years is a prime example of God working in human history. No wonder Jesus chose to use this Last Supper on the very day of the Passover feast. Do we really believe this was a coincidence? There are no accidents in life, things happen for a reason. We are all connected, but we see when we open the ears of the Spirit and listen. Therefore, God says I stand at the door and knock, if anybody opens the door I will come into his or her life (Rev. 3:20). We must be the action makers. God will force nothing on us. He gave us the ability to create and choose, which requires free will. We make choices.

In an insightful book, *We're all Doing Time,* Bo Lozoff shares a view of the three aspects of God. known to Christians as the Father, Son and Holy Ghost, stating:

> *"The three keys which activate spiritual transformation are Grace (Father), Spirit (Holy Spirit), and Effort (Sori)."*

Grace is everything-- the Holy Spirit is the force and energy of life, and Effort is the Son/Daughter or action maker. This may seem as though it is a simplistic way of viewing the essence of the Creator, but it encompasses all of what we see and also what we do not see in the world.

Dag Hammarskjold. Secretary of the United Nations said:

"In our era, the road to holiness necessarily passes through the world of action."

This is the very essence of God. Faith put into right action.

When I was about 11 years old and venturing out on my own I began to question many things. There were so many rules no wonder so many of us shied away from anything religious. For example, if you didn't fast or ate breakfast before communion you were committing a sin. Nobody ever told us that fasting was a form of soul talk with our own spirit. Sin was anything that you were told was wrong. And then there were mortal sins. If you didn't go to church on special occasions or ate meat on Friday during Lent or on Holy days of obligation you were a sinner. No wonder I believed that God was a punishing God. As far back as I can remember people were always telling kids they were bad. Bad was then associated with being a sinner. Who needed that kind of God or religion? Eventually, going to church became Sunday breakfast at the diner with a few friends where the real discussion of life would take place. Whose father beat them or whose mother was beaten or what was right and wrong to do. Who was caught stealing gum from the dime store? Or whose father had dirty pictures. Whose father was a drinker? What about the girls in the neighborhood who were friendly?

At 13 years old I was so impressed with being part of the grownup life that I would eventually go to work at a gas station cleaning tools for $1.00 an hour for three hours after school. After working there several months and thinking everything was fine, I did not realize I was the target of one of the owner's perversions. Many times, he would take me for a ride in the car and ask me if I wanted to learn how to drive or stop at the store and buy me a soda or a sandwich. I just thought he was being a decent boss and showing me his appreciation of my good work. Then after about six months when I really believed that although he was my boss, he was also my friend, he told me he had to pick up something from the parts store, and that I should take a ride with him. On the way he told me that he had to stop at his house also. I didn't think anything of it. He invited me inside for a cold soda. Once inside and relaxed he showed me some girlie magazines as I was drinking my soda. It was then that he sexually molested me. I couldn't tell anybody what had happened. I was scared and thought it was somehow my fault. I was afraid to tell my father. I don't know what he would have done. Today I have learned and realize that this was the beginning of keeping my feelings deep within myself and my eventual inability to deal with emotions, which I had compacted within myself over many years. I now see the repressed hate I held inside for so long. Although I never shared this experience with my friends on Sunday mornings at the diner, many of the other issues we had to deal with were discussed. These were the real issues of life we faced while growing up. Church on Sunday did not deal with these issues, so what good was church or religion. It only made you feel guilty. Yet somewhere in the back of my mind I was told Jesus was God and yet I never forgot what Jesus said. "I call you friends." How could this be? If Jesus was God, he was a different God from the one that punished.

Today, I find Jesus' words so clear.

> *"Ye are my friends,* **if ye do whatsoever I command you".** *Henceforth I call you not servants: for the servant knoweth not what his lord doeth: but I call you friends; for all things that I have heard of my Father I have made known unto you"*
> (John 15:15).

More than ever, God is telling us that He loves us and that we are His children. I didn't know that back then. When people no longer hear or listen to God's voice, calamity is sure to emerge. Not from God, but from humankind's inability to live a spiritual life in union with God (Jer. 8:12-14). Humankind brings punishment upon itself. God is there to carry us over the rough spots. The poem *Footprints in the Sand*[2] says it beautifully. When we are in trouble there are only one set of footprints, as God is carrying us.

William Penn, a Quaker said:

> *"True Godliness does not turn men out of the world but enables them to live better in it and excites their endeavors to mend it."*

It is sometimes easy to believe that if we feed a man a fish, we have done what is right in a social sense, believing that we have prevented him from starving. But if we feed him for only one day, tomorrow he will be hungry again. It is better to teach a man how to fish, for then you have given him the ability to feed himself for the rest of his life.[3]

St. Irenaens, Bishop of Lyons said:

"The glory of God is the living human being."

As the youngest of three children, I was often denied the opportunity to break new ground within the family setting. I guess I was spared the guilt of committing more sins, as my brother or sister were usually the ones who caught the brunt of resistance to change. They were the disobedient ones in the turbulent sixties. As mentioned, life was uneventful and the belief in a fair and just world was taken for granted, notwithstanding the punishing God syndrome (sin) always being held over your head. Who was going to heaven and who was going to hell? Having personally experienced prejudice in a small way because of my Sicilian heritage, there was a naive belief on my part that everybody lived about the same. This attitude was reinforced by the lack of any exposure to people who were different and those who were oppressed. Even within my own neighborhood, which had about 100 homes, I did not see much of a difference between families. As the neighborhood paperboy, I knew most all the families and it seemed that we all lived about the same. Reflecting today on those times past I now see the prejudice, racism and discrimination that was hurled against one or two families by many of the people that lived in the neighborhood. I have always thought that I was not small minded in my ideas but as of late I realize that, because of my contextual life experience. I see myself as sheltered. As I look back, I remember certain families being treated differently. Although I do not believe that I ever did anything against them personally. I remember somehow being made aware that these families were different. If my memory serves me correctly one family was Jewish and another extremely poor. Because they rarely cut their lawn or kept the place orderly like most other families they were singled out and ostracized.

I guess you could say that many of the neighborhood people were trying to maintain and keep up with the Jones' way of life. I know my own mom felt that way and so our house was in line with the amenities that everybody else had. In fact, this was a basis of arguments in our family. Everybody was competing on the block to keep up with everybody else. I never remember people doing anything to hurt these families, however just the fact that they felt as though they were not accepted must have been a heavy burden to bear. This was surely not an example of Jesus' teaching to love thy neighbor. In general, most people did get along with each other. Yet today I see this as one of the parables that Jesus taught. If you love those who love you. So, what. It is Jesus' teaching to love all people, looking at the spiritual essence within instead of the physical or material aspects of human existence. The unconditional love that Jesus tried to explain in His parables is why He was a spiritual genius, and His religion is one of the soul.

When I was about eleven or twelve years old, I remember one day walking with my friend Gary across a parking lot and having heard curse words, decided that I would utter one. In anticipation I was getting ready for a bolt of lightning to come down from above and consume me. I mean that was what I had been taught. Alter saying the curse word and still being alive it was now free rein to curse whenever I wanted, as this God I had been told would punish seemed as though he wasn't listening that day or wasn't really interested. I do not mean to imply that I did not or do not believe in God. I just never had a personal understanding of what God expects and His ability to speak directly to me. It has taken me almost 45 years to understand that we can never know God fully from a human perspective or consciousness until we realize and accept that we are truly Sons/Daughters of God.

Although neither Mom nor Dad read the Bible or attended church functions other than on Sunday. I am convinced they understood most of God's teachings through the Spirit. That is the very question which brings up for discussion my belief that Jesus showed us a way of life that could be filled abundantly with happiness, but religion, even the Christian religion has polluted His teaching. When we base all our belief in the hereafter and forget about those who labor under a heavy yoke in the here and now we have failed to hear God speaking to us. Both my parents were hard working respecters of the secular law and what I understood as the religious law. I never remember them using curse words or behaving in ways that would seem unacceptable to anybody back then or today. My parents tried to help others and teach their children that kind of compassion, but I do not remember them making the effort to invite those people who were poor or different over to our house for a meal. Do not take this wrong. I am not saying that my parents were bad people, the contrary is true, they tried to live a good life, but I think that that is part of the problem today. We live this human experience as the most important part of life when the spiritual life should be the most important.

It is always easier to close one's ears and eyes to the plight of others that are different than we are because we are looking at the physical instead of the spiritual. We fail to see the commonality of our spirit life connected to God and one another. Failing to take responsibility for our actions and blaming God for what does not go right is not spiritual living, but an indication that we do not yet understand this existence from a spiritual basis.

CHAPTER 4
SOCIAL RESPONSIBILITY

Having been privileged to listen to Mark L. Chapman preach and teach at the New York Theological Seminary extension program at Sing Sing prison, I have been blessed. In Chapman's book *Christianity on Trial*, he opens for review a series of questions, addressing African American religious thought, and a well portrayed glimpse of Christian historical analysis by black theologians. In my view this is of critical importance as to why Christianity teaches a different message then what Jesus taught. Our religious leaders are too concerned with money and how many people attend our churches, instead of looking to solve the spiritual sickness in our midst. I believe therefore Jesus had a clear affinity for those who were oppressed by the dominant society and the religious institutions.

Chapman quotes the Philadelphia Council of Black Clergy in a 1968 statement, which says:

> *"Aware of the oppressive role* **institutional Christianity** *has played in the African American experience, the Philadelphia clergy reminded the black church that its* **commitment is to Christ and not to Christianity,** *and that Christ was a revolutionary figure dedicated to the eradication of exploitative[1] and oppressive systems."*

Chapman goes on to state that Calvin Marshall, a leader in the National Council of Black Churches (NCBC), believed that:

> *"Jesus was a radical leader who confronted the religious, political, and social systems that oppressed the poor."*[2,3]

Chapman next discusses Albert Cleage, who, like Howard Thurman, was a defender of the Christian faith albeit in a vastly different way, but nonetheless in a way depicting the Jesus of the Bible as a Black Nationalist leader whose mission was like Malcolm X.

Cleage stated:

> *"Jesus didn't spend His life waiting to be crucified. Instead, he devoted His life to two important tasks: Organizing the Black Nation to fight against Roman rule, while preaching against the spirit of individualism that corrupted His people, many of whom were willing to sell out the Nation for personal gain.*
>
> *Jesus was distorted by the institution (Christianity) that was set up in His name; The Apostle Paul...set up Churches everywhere and spoke. This is Christianity. All of you who follow after Jesus, come right on in here. And then he changed the whole thing around. No longer was it building a Nation, it was tearing down a Nation. It was leading the people right back to the same old individualistic kind of thing that Jesus had fought against all of His life. In the name of Jesus, they created a new kind of individualism."*

Cleage believed that the Old Testament and the synoptic gospels as preached by Jesus were concerned about humankind's condition in the here and now, and that salvation was a part and parcel of how we live. I agree. This is the difference between Institutional Christianity (Slave Theology) and the teachings and liberation of Jesus. Jesus was concerned about the condition of men and women here and now first, then in salvation, as the two go hand in hand when the life of the spirit is born within.

It is my understanding and belief that black theology and liberation theology have begun the dismantling of Christianity theologically, and have allowed the teachings of Jesus to be recognized for what they are. In this way we can begin to understand how to speak with God and realize who we are, Children of God.

The following statement by Gayraud Wilmore is instructive for liberation of all peoples, keeping in mind a Christian faith based on Jesus' teachings, not Institutional Christianity,

> *"The Christian faith not only transcends ultimately the ethnocentric culture of the white man, but that of the black man as well; that this Christ, in whom there is neither Jew nor Greek, bond nor free, is also neither black nor white."*

Today, I am convinced that Dr. Chapman is a follower of Jesus. Dr. Chapman has crossed the boundary of religiosity and allows that of God to speak from the depths of his soul. Dr. Chapman as an African American has firsthand experience of the type of oppression people suffer. In putting Christianity on Trial, I believe Chapman has proved my point conclusively. Jesus has been shown to be the truth, and Christianity the "religion" has been found guilty, failing to nurture the spiritual health of all those who call themselves Christian. We have forgotten the teachings of Jesus to love one another. This cannot be done with the mouth but must be done through action.

In a book by Joseph F. Girzone. *Joshua and the City*, the author uses the fictional character of Joshua to expose part of the answer. The following statement expresses what I am trying to say about Christianity not being Jesus' religion.

Joshua says:

> *"Many of those children are geniuses but are not college material. Their genius dies in their breast because no one cares. The anger, crime, the drugs, are expressions of their frustrations. Locking them up in prison is not the answer. They need to be given hope. The neglect of political leaders and business leaders (religious leaders) in not aiding them to lead productive lives is just as criminal as the behavior of the young people in the streets. If you don't imprison the one, why imprison the other. Prison is not a solution. It is the government's admission of failure to solve a problem. After a person's release from prison, the same environment still exists, and still demands a solution. That solution is development of young people's talents and the providing of jobs for them so they can develop a sense of pride in themselves."*

The above problem would not exist today if we were Jesus followers, because then we would all be responsible for one another as it was in the first century. Therefore, we are at war all over the world. We fail to see the soul-ship common to us all. Otherwise, God's spirit would move and fill each living soul and they would know that they are children of the Creator and connected to one another. This is why it is so important to hold our society and ourselves responsible for our youth, they are our future. This is why we must dismantle religious institutions and governments that oppress the God within us all. I am not saying that this is not happening today as men and women struggle for change, it is. But society must open their eyes and become more involved.

Many people throughout the world are concerned about crime, the environment, morality, injustice, the plight of the poor, the suffering of the innocent, and all *"those who stand with their backs to the wall."*[3] But many have also fallen asleep and no longer believe we can make change. We have forgotten or do not understand who we are. But there is hope, men and women are speaking out and trying to make a difference. We must do the same. When we see wrong, we must expose it. If we know the government is violating the law, we must come together in spiritual unity of love and find ways to change that which is wrong.[4]

As Dostoyevsky once said

"Our prisons are a reflection of our society."

My own personal experience of being in prison has opened my eyes to a whole new world. Prison life is about routine: each day like the one before; each week like the one before it, so that the months and years blend into each other. Anything that departs from this pattern upsets the authorities, for routine is the sign of a well-run prison. Routine is also comforting for the prisoner, which is why it can be a trap. Routine can be a pleasant habit which becomes hard to resist, for routine makes the time go faster. Losing a sense of time is an easy way to lose one's grasp on life and even one's sanity. Time slows down in prison; the days seem endless if idleness and inactivity are allowed to be the master. Even when busy, time each day seems to go slowly. What might take a few hours to accomplish on the outside in the real world may take months or even years to accomplish on the inside. Minutes at times seem like hours yet the years sometimes in retrospect seem like minutes. Before you know it, days become years and you can't figure out where the years have gone. Each day is a day of survival and the challenge to figure a way out legally through the courts and healthfully through good eating and godly behavior. However, that is only a dream as each day behind the wall has a detrimental psychological effect we are rarely aware of. Friendships and physical contact between human beings is superficial and frowned upon by the authorities. To emerge from prison without the psyche being diminished and unaffected before the prison experience took place is impossible. Studies that have been conducted about prisoners incarcerated for crimes, and prisoners of war show that both experience the detrimental effects of prison.[5] The goal each day is to stay alive. Learning the prison routine and nuances of prison life is especially important. Something as simple as using an empty toothpaste tube as a spoon is a learning experience. Coming to terms with the prison administration's function is particularly important in order to have a strategy and develop a plan of survival. Prison is designed to take away a person's identity, break the spirit, and eliminate a person's understanding of who they are. Every form of psychological manipulation is used to let a prisoner know that they are considered as nothing but a number. The invisibleness of being, is a unique experience, which will be discussed later. Individuality is taken away so that every person in green (the color of clothes issued to all New York State prisoners) is a group to be identified as "nobodies". If it were possible the authorities' goal would be to stamp out the spark of the Divine that makes each of us human and spiritually able to know who we are. Unfortunately, this does happen to some, as their spirit is broken. They find themselves sustained in psychiatric units mesmerized with prescription drugs.

Yet sharing with another prisoner is almost nonexistent. The prison atmosphere is one of suspicion and everybody has his or her own problems. A comment made in confidence to one man may end up causing problems later during his incarceration. Therefore, very few prisoners confide in one another. As important is the feeling of loss. Men are transferred with no advance notice. A person may have known someone for years, exercised or shared meals together, then all of a sudden, they are gone. This can be devastating, yet it is common. As a result, prisoners tend to stay by themselves. The lack of self-esteem alters a lifetime of being told you are inferior or less than a human being is devastating. Many men of all ages in prison who cannot read or write are afraid to tell anybody for fear of being further ostracized. That is why gang membership both inside and outside prison is rising. Gang members are accepted for what they are and then used. This makes them feel as though they belong and are important. They survive on a false sense of being needed and of having value. Lack of the ability for our young to share their deepest feelings leads to anger and hate and results in the violence we see common among our young people in all walks of life. No wonder young people have an "I don't care attitude" and want to "get theirs" no matter how they must behave. We cannot put a Band-Aid on our feelings. We must begin to share what we feel in our hearts. Whatever troubles our spirit has a direct relationship on our physical being. We must be able to internalize our lives and take a deep breath. Yoga teaches us to concentrate on our breath. Remember life is only one breath away.

In my own life, prison has forced me to see who I am. This has been difficult but nonetheless the most important experience and revelation of my life. I have come to know who I am and how to communicate with God. I remember when I was at the County jail and involved in a special program started by an ex- offender and called D.A.R.T. (Drug and Alcohol Rehabilitation Treatment). The DART program allowed men and women to understand what and how their lives have been affected because of drugs and alcohol. During my participation in the DART program, spirituality was an important aspect of understanding why we used substances to affect us. Today I see clearly how important this was. It was the first time in my life that someone was telling me that God was a loving God, and not a punishing God. In *Of Water and the Spirit*, Malidoma Patrice Some gives an admirable personal explanation of the way Christian missions would kidnap young men in Africa in the name of religion. Unfortunately, this is an example of what institutional religion has done to Jesus' teachings.

Each day as I look out the window of my prison cell, Lady Hudson lazily meanders past Sing Sing Correctional Facility, once known as the place "up the river" an infamous bastion of punishment. The Hudson carries a flotilla of water vessels carrying people who hope to get a glimpse of another world inhabited by the convict on the other side of life's fences. Yet there exists a commonality between all human beings, for many that are imprisoned are free, while others suffer a worse imprisonment outside the physical walls. Daily the eerie sound of gunshots can be heard in the background, as Correctional Officers' practice using all manner of guns, while at the same time the tap tap tap of typewriter keys can be heard in the Law Library. And so, on one side of the fence there are those who practice the art of warfare with weapons and on the other side those who practice the art of warfare with legal papers submitted to the Courts as the war for justice continues. It is these very men and women who are now labeled as convicts who keep the law in a state of flux so the government does not overstep its bounds. No wonder the government encourages the media to write negative reports about prisoners who litigate. Most people fail to realize that jailhouse lawyers are the very last vanguards that uphold the rights of those who are free.

I do not posit the idea that we do not need law and order, but we must realize that since the beginning of time and the birth of consciousness human beings have made mistakes.

Without jailhouse lawyers the government would have free reign to lock up all those who do not fit the mold. Even today as government cries about prison litigation and its frivolity, 213 new prisons were built over the last 5 years. Jailhouse lawyers then are one of the last vestiges of a republic built on a Constitution, which guarantees the rights of many. In God we Trust. If the government is successful in denying access to the Courts for prisoners, who will champion the cause for Truth. Justice and Equality for all? It is the exceedingly difficult job of our courts to decide what is correct, yet prisoner litigation is the very impetus that guides our understanding of what the community, society, and our country believes is just punishment. Jailhouse lawyers may be viewed as a necessary evil, but without access to the courts, the balance of government power will run rampant. The present situation is that after serving many years in prison and trying to do everything possible to change one's life, one is not let out of prison. Political pressures are the reason whether a person is released or kept in prison after serving the sentence given by the judge. Men and women who have changed their lives have become victims of the Prison mentality and are now Political Prisoners. Billions of dollars are being spent even though crime is down. New prisons are being built in communities that have helped to elect politicians and are now being paid back for their votes. This is wrong. Public relation companies are brainwashing our society to believe what the government wants them to embrace. That poor people are a threat to white America. Racism is pervasive. It has nothing to do with personal change or transformation. This is criminal. Those without sin cast the first stone. Many people cannot relate to the denial of parole, having never experienced such a procedure. Talking from a personal point of view, one might ask "What is it like?" To say the least it is a devastating and sobering occurrence. After working towards the specific day for many years, you face two or three Parole Board commissioners, who hold your fate in their hands. It is an awesome power the commissioners have when it affects your ability to move on with your life. After working 13 years with the belief that there is a system of justice, it is a stark awakening that it is not true. An example of this is our belief that a human being can change, redemption. For some men or women denial of parole is sometimes the point of no return and breaks their spirit. For those who have prepared themselves for a denial of parole, it is no less devastating, but moving on is a must. Although I find it difficult to swallow, stumbling blocks are the steppingstones on the road to our future.

The story below is how most people in prison and many outside feel because they do not know who they are. I am only one person who has had to deal with this, but my explanation is based on my own contextual walk in life. The ability to look deep within at our soul connection regardless of our physical or ideological differences is a gift. We are all related to the family of God.

An example of this is my own experience. Although I have

never lost a child, I have lost significant others who I loved dearly. When I first realized that I had caused two people to lose their lives I believed I was the worst person who ever lived. I suffered nightmares and felt as though I was nothing.

For me, the experience reminded me of the time when I was divorced. Having been married for almost 10 years the suddenness and finality of that breakup left me devastated. It is never easy to deal with life when it touches the very core of our being, that of the soul. The Spirit and the soul are different but connected like a drop of water from the ocean which we return to after this physical existence ends. Each operating on their own plane of existence.

I remember having to force myself to eat, as I did not have an appetite. The whole world seemed to be a foreign place. I felt as though I was all alone and that nobody could understand what I was going through or could help. All I wanted to do was sleep. That was an exceedingly difficult endeavor. Many nights I would toss and turn all night long until the morning light shone through the window and I would fall asleep from sheer exhaustion only to be woken by the alarm clock for work. I would have to force myself to work as I had no other source of income. I did not even have a place to sleep other than my van. It was a difficult time in my life, and it took several months to live through this experience and move forward. Appearing before the Parole board was remarkably similar. After preparing for that day for many years, the night before was sleepless, going over in my mind what I would say. I knew how sorry I was for what had happened, but sometimes saying sorry does not convey how deeply you feel. Throughout my incarceration I have tried to show people by my actions the sorrow in my heart, thereby making amends for what I had done. Even though knowing in the spirit that you have done everything that was in your power the appearance before the parole board is terror. Knowing that even if you are denied it is not because of anything that you have not done. This may be comforting as it allows you to say to yourself, well if I get denied it is not my fault. The days after appearance are also filled with anxiety in that you wonder what the decision will be. You see a decision is made as soon as you leave the room, but you are not told for anywhere between 3 and 7 days later. This is a horrible practice. This adds to the suffering and the agony of not knowing after a lifetime of waiting to appear before the board. I have often thought that my own agony reflects the agony, pain, and emotional hurt that I caused the victim's families. I wish it could be different. Maybe that is how we come to understand how our behavior affects others, when it happens to us. No experience in life may be the same but if we are open to the spirit within, we can feel other people's hurts. Of course, for every person the parole board is different. Yet I have seen men devastated due to lack of spiritual strength. For those men I have tried to console them after they have raised their hopes about being released only to be told they are denied. Interestingly, the person who has done nothing doesn't expect much and is usually not affected as deeply. Can much be expected?

How many of us have looked forward to our first date or the hope of meeting a young lady and that person not showing up. The feelings are quite bothersome. For those who are denied parole it is a situation that we would not want our friends, family, loved ones, or even our enemies to experience. This last time going to the parole board I could not bring myself to tell my mom I was even going. Knowing the usual procedure when a case is reversed. I did not want to put my mother through the devastating effects of being denied again. Another aspect of this whole farce is the appeal process. After months of waiting, it is usually the case that parole appeal is denied almost 100% of the time at the administrative level. How else could it operate when the very same people who have denied you parole are the very same people who decide the appeal. Few people after deciding will reverse themselves. Yet many of these decisions are overturned by the court sometimes one or two years later when it is time to go back to the parole board again. Even the courts are leery about letting people go and the only decision they usually make is sending the person back for another parole board and again going through the illegal proceeding. The Executive department of government has the impression that they are above the law. At the last parole appearance when I brought up the fact that there were illegal procedures being used the commissioner told me in no uncertain terms that she didn't care what the parole manual said that this is the way it was being done. The courts have recently informed me that they will not hold the parole commissioners responsible for violations of the law because they have absolute immunity. This is wrong and must be changed. If we are willing to go before the parole board with our tail between our legs and hope for justice without opening our mouth, then nothing will ever change. There is a time for us to stand up for what is right. What I learned from this experience however was the way my behavior afterwards was looked upon by others. How could I be an Inspiration for others to see? We live in a nation that was originally based on principles of forgiveness and the ability of people to be redeemed, unfortunately we no longer stand on those virtues. We view punishment as the answer to anyone who makes a mistake.

J. Hudson Taylor who founded the China Inland Mission understood that our connection to God was experiential. He said:

"Oh friends! When we are brought into the position of having practical fellowship with God in trial and sorrow and suffering, we leant a lesson that is not to be learned amid ordinary life. This is why God so often brings us through trying experiences."

There is however an unspoken network within the prison so that prisoners know when something is going to happen. When a search will take place or a lock down. Therefore, prison authorities have outlawed unions and regular prison gatherings. Many times, plans and proposals that are submitted to the administration that have a common theme for an event are scrutinized and denied. Prison officials are against organized groups for fear of unity. The prison administration's greatest tool is keeping prisoners at each other and unorganized. Prison officials are concerned about common causes. This is why among prisoners; men with different gifts and capabilities try to help others lift themselves up, becoming stronger through the process. At one time the older prisoners would be role models for new prisoners entering the system, but today the mentality of prisoners has changed. Now the authorities have put into place behavioral psychological tools to control people. Tools such as commissary, television, radios, and a large number of female officers are used to control and entice the senses.

Prison authorities would be the first ones to admit that prisoners run prisons. This is true if everything runs smoothly. Prisoners do most of the work maintaining the prison structure as well as keeping prisoners clothed and fed. Prison industries produce billions of dollars of goods at prison wages that amount to 15 cents an hour. Slave labor. Clearly prisons represent modem day slavery with permission from the government to carry on exploitation of the masses. Prisons today are filled with confidential informants letting the authorities know exactly what is going on. Once prisoners become complacent and submit to oppression and domination of prison authorities their sense of humanness is taken away. As a result, attitudes of self-hatred and rejection for other prisoners becomes reified. Prisoners begin to see themselves as victims of the system and feed into the belief that they are incapable of transforming themselves. This perpetuates the conditions that exist. This is where the teachings of Jesus, Mohammed, Moses, Malcolm, Martin Luther King, Jr., Gandhi, and others are so important. These great spiritual leaders understood how the spirit could transcend violence. Whether we are in prison or outside, when we see wrong, we must expose that wrong. If we do not do something, we are just as guilty for allowing the wrong to continue. We must come together and hear that of God calling us all, instead oi dividing ourselves with religious dogma and institutional religiosity. We do not need another Attica. Selma, Montgomery and Atlanta but must be willing to change these wrongs before they erupt. What we need is more "Million-man marches" of all people.

If we look at history as a precursor for the future, the handwriting is on the wall. We eliminate college education in prison to keep young men and women ignorant so we can continue to build prisons. This must stop. We spend more money on prisons than we do on educating our youth.[6] This is wrong. People can only be exploited and oppressed for so long. People were drinking and partying up until the days of the flood even though Noah warned them. Are we on the same path today? Look around and if you have ears, listen. Why are our youth killing? We listen to the news and for the most part, it is negative. Why don't we hear about the miracles[7] that take place every day in our world? Why do we look to shows like *Highway to Heaven* and *Ally McBeal* to hear about spiritual experiences? It is time to stand up and be counted. We must do something. Will we sit back until they put everybody in prison because of their color or culture? Will we allow the government to continue to build 150 new prison cells a day? Can we allow the government to divert hundreds of millions of dollars from education, welfare, hospital care, and social programs to prison construction? Do we want to help perpetuate this Prison mentality by allowing our children to be targeted for failure? We must begin to see that those men and women who made a mistake and have changed their lives while in prison should be considered for release and parole. These men and women who have gone to college and realized the error of their ways need to be back in our communities to help each other. If Parole Board practices are illegal, then we must find ways to non-violently upset the program. Who needs parole commissioners that make $76,500.00 plus a car, travel expenses, lodging, etc. if everybody gets denied parole because of political pressure from the Governor, no matter how much they have changed their lives? Men and women in prison have become political prisoners. Why do we need parole commissioners if their job is to deny everyone parole no matter the circumstances? Unfortunately, it is all about big business and the money to be made. Our government no longer cares about human beings who are minorities or people who do not fit their mold. Yet government spends more money on prison than on educating our young. And even that education is superficial. We fail to teach our children about the real issues of life. Teachers are one of the lowest paid professional jobs in our country. Do we care? We have our priorities backwards. We need to start talking to one another and dealing with our inner feelings. No wonder our children feel alienated; they have no one to talk with about their feelings. The family structure is so nuclear we need to create avenues of communication about our soul experience. This is a problem both in prison and on the outside. Even so although communication between people inside prison and their families is so important, the five free letters per week to keep people in touch with their families has been eliminated by government indifference. This is wrong. The struggle in prison is to be recognized as a human being with self-worth and is a microcosm of those in society who struggle against oppression by government. Prison has become big business no longer concerned with rehabilitation or punishment, but the warehousing and support of human inventory. Welfare of the nineties has become prison. The prisons have become big business with human beings as livestock. This is why it is so important for the prisoners to see the ruse and look within at their own Godliness and stand up for what is right.

Our leaders see prisons as warehousing of human stock. Money has become the dominant force, the God of materiality. Prison rehabilitation is no longer a penological goal. But punishment is used in a psychological way with the threat of violence against one's person. People have become the product. Our courts turn a blind eye to injustice. Morality is dead. Even our president does not respect the office of honor. It is time for us to respect and realize each other's soul existence. There is also a very subtle problem with prison religious organizations in that they are here to keep the peace. Very few religious people who are part of the prison authority are willing to put their head on the chopping block when they see wrong, because they are employed by the State. This is their livelihood. Many are similar in their actions to the Pharisees and Sadducees in Jesus' time. They do not want to put their positions in jeopardy. As with every other institution there is a blue wall of silence. There is also a problem with religious groups that come into the facilities. Nobody wants to rock the boat like Jesus did. It is one thing to be concerned about a man or woman's spirituality but what about the injustice that is common each day both in prison and our society. Correctional Officer and Police brutality, illegal confinement, inadequate medical care, sexual harassment, intimidation, etc. etc. not to mention the abuse that families must put up with when they come to visit.

This is where we can learn a great lesson from Jesus. Jesus challenged the very societal norms. Unfortunately, modem day spiritual leaders who have done the same, like Jesus, have lost their lives. Present day political agenda is an evil so large and pervasive that without unity and masses of people coming together it is too big for any one person to change and correct. This is where the spiritual teachings and genius of Jesus are realized if embraced.

In *Beyond the Whiteness of Whiteness*, Jane Lazarre expresses how our keeping quiet hurts us all:

> *"You speak out against even the smallest injustice, whoever you are, especially, if you are in a position of privilege, especially when the injustice is not directed, for the moment perhaps, at you. You don't have to be black to realize that African and African American thought and experience is essential for all people to learn if we want to understand the truth of what happened to this world over the first few centuries, truths which landed us in the violent and truly alarming times in which we find ourselves today."*

Today I realize that we go through trials and tribulations in our lives to strengthen our faith, and to understand the essence of God within. Each day is a learning experience and a blessing, being given the opportunity to make this world a better place.

CHAPTER 5
LIFE LEARNING

As I think back to my own family I think of my father's life and realize that he was in tune with God even though he really didn't understand it.[1] Although I never thought much about it then, I knew he was a good man and father. I sometimes wonder where that came from and believe it was from his mother, the grandmother I never had the opportunity to meet. As the oldest son in a family of three growing up in the depression years my father's life was filled with responsibility at an incredibly early age. Then when it finally seemed as though his dream of attaining a college education became a reality, that dream was cut short. As a man who earned a scholarship to Pratt institute in 1933 no easy task, the loss of that opportunity due to my father's father being hospitalized must have been a severe blow. As the oldest son he was responsible for the family's well-being and had to leave school after one year. Only a short time later the loss of my father's mother must have been a devastating event to experience. I have been left with the sincere conviction that this was a difficult and life changing experience for my father. It is no surprise that my father was so concerned about one of his own children going to college. And although it came at an extremely late stage of his life, I am the only one that fulfilled my father's dream. Likewise, it has come at an extremely high price and in a very strange circumstance, but I am a firm believer that God plants us where we bloom best even though that is hard to understand in the beginning of our circumstance. A difficult but fond memory is when my father came to see me after I was sentenced and before I was sent to the State system. In the visiting room he took my hand and said no matter what I love you; things happen in life. I then made the promise to him that I would try and get a college education. Even though it took eleven years, that dream of his became a reality when in 1995 I graduated from Marist College. Eventually, I would also earn a master's degree from New York Theological Seminary. Unfortunately, my father would pass on into the spiritual realm before I graduated, but he was grateful for what I had accomplished. To say the least I can never change what has happened, only try and live a good life whether in prison or outside to show how sorry I am for what I did.

Many people claim that we have the written word (the Bible) and that is all that we need. Unfortunately, the written word was transformed from the spoken word, and therefore it may be suspect. There were no computers or recorders back then. Having personally studied the Bible at seminary I know that some parts of the Bible are in different languages and styles. And so, we cannot be 100% sure of the accuracy. That statement may offend many people, yet we know that words are only symbols.

Words are the least accurate form of communication due to the contextual analysis people perceive themselves to live in. This may have a significant effect on the translation. This means that communication with God, in its most accurate form should be directly in God's language. If people said they heard voices with their physical ears, and it was God speaking to them in the English language, society and even religious people would consider them lunatics. At the same time if we said we were listening to God with ears of the spirit we would also be considered lunatics to those who do not know God. If you have ears listen (Matt 11:15). This is a profound statement when we realize that the human condition has separated us from knowing our soul, which is the spirit of God manifest on the physical plane. Can any of us imagine being lost and when our parents found us, we would say, I was speaking to God and some friends.

These are clear signs telling us we are Sons and Daughters of God. Yet we split hairs over spiritual teaching if it is not about religion. We must begin to look at the condition of each human being's inward center as the crucial arena where the issues would determine the destiny of humankind in our world today. We have a direct line to speak and listen to God. If we only understand He speaks a language that we have forgotten or will not believe we can speak. For a long time, we have been told that God is somewhere else and very distant, when we are a part of God's wholeness. I would be the first to admit that if someone spoke to me in sign language I would not understand. I would first have to learn that language. Speaking with God and listening to God in His language must be remembered. We have forgotten from lack of practice. Why is it said so often out of the mouth of babes comes wisdom? They still remember how to speak God's language. We have not brainwashed them or caused them to doubt that God speaks directly with us.

I remember a time so vividly when my daughter Anna and I were sitting at a diner having dinner. This was shortly after the separation between my wife Bonnie and I. It had been an exceedingly difficult week for us all. Anna at eight years old took my hand in her hand and said:

> *"Don't worry Dad I know it is not easy, we all stumble, but remember, God is right there to pick us up."*

This child of God could hear God's voice, and at that time I wasn't fully listening. Out of the mouth of babes' truth is spoken. I will always cherish this memory.

Jesus made it clear that when God talks to us He talks to us in His language, which is rarely the spoken word we hear with our ears.

> *"And Jesus lifted up His eyes, and said, Father, I thank thee that thou hast heard me. And I knew that thou hearest me always: but because of the people that stand by I said it, that they may believe that thou hast sent me. And when he had thus spoken, he cried with a loud voice, Lazarus, come forth"* (John 11:41-44).

This is an intense statement. It shows that even before Jesus had called out the name of Lazarus, he had already spoken with the Divine. Jesus knew what the results would be but for the people present he said it out loud in their language. This is a perfect example of Jesus showing us the unspoken communication between God and in faith our ability to receive what we ask. Our thoughts have tremendous power. They are real.

> *"If you have faith as a grain of mustard seed. ...nothing shall be impossible unto you"* (Matthew 17: 20-21).

Jesus is telling us we have a direct line to the Creator that is the Spirit of God within, Enlightenment, Inner peace. Inner Light. Nirvana, etc. It really does not matter if we name our connection to God. What does matter is our personal knowledge of that connection and the peace, love and courage it takes to know who we are and live beyond the human existence, embracing the spiritual essence within. Jesus said we are born of the spirit when our lives begin to exhibit love, joy, peace, longsuffering, gentleness, goodness, faith, meekness, temperance, and we live a life in union with God. We must not be so concerned with whether Jesus said this or that, or Mohammed, or Buddha, but the Spirit of truth born within us will guide us in right living.

This should not be a surprise, for Jesus said:

> *"I thank thee, O Father, Lord of Heaven and earth, because thou hast hid these things from the wise and prudent, and hast revealed them unto babes"[2] (Matthew: 11: 25).*

Why is communicating with God directly so hard for us to accept? Do we limit God? One reason may be that we have been taught that God spoke and inspired men of old to write the Bible and then God just decided to stop talking. We must remember that communication with God must be understood in the context of where we are in life, and through soul talk.

As Gutierrez explains,

> *"When two lovers fall silent and simply remain in each other's presence, they know that they are experiencing love of each other at a deeper level."*

Spirituality is a very intimate experience. As sexual being's soul talk is a language we have never acknowledged but experienced when we join both physically and spiritually. How few of us take the time to enjoy each other's physical form? When we are intimate it should be an incredibly special and rewarding time. On many occasions I have spent several hours with scented oil massaging and enjoying the physical form of woman. This is an incredible sharing for both people. This is an unbelievably beautiful preparation for the wonder of joining together both physically and spiritually. We as humans have moved away from our[2] sensuality, which God gave us above all other creatures. We should learn to enjoy it. If we share our feelings with our children, then we won't worry so much about teen pregnancy and promiscuousness. We need to take away the taboos about sex and discuss our God manifest essence in the physical form.

Clearly this is a paradox, yet it is a process attained by knowing that we are of the essence of God. That in silence God will talk with us in His language and we can talk with our Creator.

St. Thomas Aquinas once said:

> *"Every truth without exception - and whoever may utter it - is from the Holy Spirit."*

The more we understand this simple truth the more we understand God talking with us and guiding our lives. We become the vessel used by God to share His message of love. If we can only get ourselves out of the way and let the spirit within guide us, we would be living a vastly different life.

In a quite simple yet penetrating book by Richard Carlson, Ph.D *Don't sweat the Small Stuff...and it's all small stuff* Dr. Carlson in note 95 says:

> *"Many of us don't listen to our intuitive heart for fear that we couldn't possibly know something without thinking it through."*

Dr. Carlson reveals using small captions that there is much more that we know, than what we have been taught about living life simply,

> *"Are we not worth much more than birds and yet they have plenty to eat?" (Matt. 6:26).*

The religion of Jesus is to love thy God with all thy mind, body, and soul, and to love our neighbor as we love ourselves. If we say we love God but do not love our neighbor, we are liars for how can we love what we do not see (1 Pet. 1:8).

Eastern philosophers said it differently but it means the same thing. True happiness in this world comes about by loving and caring about others, whereas suffering comes about from caring for ourselves only.

The Buddha said it very simply,

> *"As the shadow follows the body, as we think, so we become."*

We are so concerned about our human experience that we forget that someday we will all die. We fear death and the spiritual existence instead of embracing death and living a life of truth, because we do not believe in the spiritual realm. Yet we must learn that nothing can separate us from the love of God for we are His children, and the creative physical manifestation of His Spirit.

In *Of Water and the Spirit,* Malidoma Some gives us an inner view to the world of the Spirit. One comment, which I find so well expressed, is his explanation to find ourselves.

> *"One must go through a process of relearning, enforcement of lessons, and the consolidation of new knowledge. This kind of education is nothing less than a return to one's true self, that is, to the divine within us."*

Zoroaster from Persia said:

> *"If we love one another, God dwells in us."*

We so treasure this life that we rarely embrace the thought of death because of the fear of the unknown. Yet we have been told that there are many mansions being prepared for us (John 14:2). Fear of the unknown is only feared when we do not have the answers. We have been given the answers but how many of us have listened? This is one of our many difficulties in living the human experience.

A contemporary Quaker named John Punshon says:

> *"That the Light of Christ (tnith) is in **everyone** regardless of their religion, culture, nationality, race or anything else."*

It is a great statement, when viewed in the light of our existence as persons made in the image of God. The problem is that many of us were never taught that we are children of God. The Kingdom of God that dwells within us all is ineffable and cannot be destroyed.

It was George Fox founder of the Society of Friends who was so moved by the inner experience that he was led to say:

> *"The Lord did gently lead me along, and did let me see His love, which was endless and eternal and **surpasses** all the knowledge that men have in the natural state or can get by history or books."*[3]

I find the statement above to be immensely powerful in that it explains how God's love surpasses all human knowledge. Some people may not yet be listening or believe in God, and so we must respect every human beings own walk in life. We may share whatever we have but we can never force anything on anybody. The parable of the seed is a perfect example of this. We may plant a seed and water it daily, but God makes it grow (1 Corinth: 3: 7-8).

Gustavo Gutierrez says it very simply:

> *"Theology will then be speech that has been enriched by silence."*

Understanding God is easy when we are listening with the ears of the spirit, our heart and mind.

This was brought to my mind in a prison Quaker meeting and today I again see God talking directly to me. One Friday evening Pete Seegar, the Folk singer, came to visit the prison. As the evening moved on Pete sang a song he wrote called a "Little Bit of This and a Little Bit of That" (Rock Soup). The song tells a story about a man who came to a poor town and set up a big pot filled with water in the middle of the village. He put branches under the pot, lit a fire, and put a rock into the pot and started boiling the water. After a few minutes, a young boy came along and asked him what he was doing. The man said he was making rock soup but that it would be a little better if he had an onion. So, the boy went off and found an onion. Sometime later another boy came along and asked the same question. In response, the man said again it would be better soup if he had a carrot. This continued for several hours as different children brought different vegetables and other things to put into the soup. Eventually the soup was finished and with a little bit of this and a little bit of that a grand pot of soup was made and fed the whole town. This modem day parable showed me how people working together could accomplish so much. As the meeting progressed, we sat in silent worship which is the normal course in Quaker meetings. During this time. I had the idea that if those of us in prison could collect a can of food from every prisoner maybe we could feed some homeless people. Strangely. I mentioned this story to one of the people at the meeting and two weeks later I received a songbook from Pete Seegar. I then mentioned it to my friend Elva whom I had met at the county jail who mentioned it to her friend Father Bill. She told me that Father Bill was a fan of Pete Seegar as he was also a banjo player. Then several weeks later I mentioned to one of the meeting leaders Dan Whitfield, a Quaker, how much Father Bill liked Pete's singing. To my surprise Pete sent Father Bill a copy of his songbook. Here was God using me to touch a person who I did not know.

The story continues several years later. In 1996 as a student of the New York Theological Seminary Master's Degree program at Sing Sing Prison. I presented to my class the idea of collecting cans as a class project to feed the homeless, as a result over 500 cans of food were collected. With the help of Rye Presbyterian Church, who would eventually match what we collected, 140 homeless families had an Easter meal at Port Chester in 1996. Since that time, every class has had a food drive. This year's class, with the help of Friends meeting houses (Quakers) and Rye Church collected over 2000 cans and were able to feed homeless people in ten different communities for Easter. This to me is the creative power of God talking directly to me. I am blessed that I now understand that so many times God was speaking to me in His language. It just took me so long to understand this because of what I had been told throughout my life. Therefore, I believe this message which God has asked me to share is so important. At that time, my understanding was that God's words, were in a book and that is as close as you got. Looking back, I would venture to say that my parents or our family were "religious" as the term was used back then or even today. I am merely stating that religion was part of growing up in a Christian family. In retrospect, I see my parents as believers in Jesus' teaching and the kind of people who tried to instill a sense of caring for others in their children. We were taught and led to believe that the most important thing that mattered was how we acted. We were not told or taught that we are all responsible for each other. If we really look at what Jesus taught, then and only then can we see that we are all brothers and sisters, and that the church is not a structure of material things but those who are followers of God. Most of us were taught as children that people were responsible for their own problems and therefore most people turned a blind eye towards all those who suffered.

> *"So, don't worry at all about having enough food and clothing. Why be like the heathen? For they take pride in all these things and are deeply concerned about them. But your heavenly Father already knows perfectly well that you need them, and he will give them to you if you give Him first place in your life and live as he wants you to. So, don't be anxious about tomorrow. God will take care of your tomorrow too. Live one day at a time"* (Matthew: 6:28).

How often we may have heard this quote when we were young and growing up but how many of us could believe it. I remember when I first started understanding the Bible when I was at the County jail and going to Bible study under Reverend Torres. Here was a man inside the belly of the beast who was happy to come in and talk with men and show them God's power. I remember talking with my sister on the phone and her asking me if I had enough money or if I needed anything. I didn't want to tell her that my entire commissary purchase had been stolen the day before. It was a choice I had to make; either go to Easter Mass and leave my cell empty or stay in my cell and protect my possessions. Anyway, I went to Mass and when I returned someone had taken a broom and went fishing in my cell. That is the jail term used when someone goes into your cell even if it is locked. I thought about what happened when I first returned and was upset, but I had received such blessings at the Easter Mass I knew in my heart I had made the right decision. I also realized that my life was changing when instead of threatening someone for stealing my stuff, I announced that whoever had taken it must have needed it more than I. I then spoke loudly that I had received greater blessings in God's words than all the possessions I had lost were worth. The conclusion of this story is that after I told my sister that I had plenty even though I had nothing, one day later a man who was not expecting to go home was told to pack up. He came to my cell and gave me two big bags of clothes, food, and a radio. Everything that had been stolen was replaced plus more. I was again awed by God's ability to show me how it works even though at the time I really didn't believe fully that God was talking to me in an experiential language. God was showing me He was present.

The following poem came from this experience.

INNER PEACE

The heart may be in prison
And yet it can be free,
No matter where the flesh
God supplies the key.

The key is the Spirit
Which opens up the door,
And fills the heart with peace
When man can do no more.

For a prison may hold our bodies
Yet bars will never keep,
The spirit of God inside us
Which love will always seek.

So, let your heart be peaceful
And trust in God's true word,
For even in a prison
God's voice can still be heard.

I remember many years after my older brother had died of cancer I was still wrestling with his death. I remember talking with a Baptist preacher who, a soft soul, I had met where I worked. I was telling him that I still didn't understand why God had taken my brother. My brother was a man who had never hurt anybody as far as I knew in his entire life. A man who had a wife and two very young children who had struggled hard to get where he was, then Bam he has cancer and dies. Is this a loving God whose justice is fair, understandable or has grace and mercy? No wonder people do not want to know that kind of God. Then my friend Knot said to me: "John try and imagine walking in an apple orchard in the middle of the summer. The apples are ripening at different stages and the smell of them is amazing. Life in its fullness is all around as butterflies, bees, and all of nature is blooming. Then when you find the apple that is the ripest and looks and smells the best you pick it. You have changed the existence of the surroundings forever. No longer is that apple part of the tree but is now on its own. So, it is like that when we understand a minute aspect of God. God does what God wants when he wants and for whatever purpose." Then Knot went on to explain, that God is like the steward of the apple orchard, and when he finds apples that are ripe, he picks them. We all ripen at different times. This simple explanation has filled a place in my being that was empty for a long time. Simple as it may sound it gave me an idea about God's ways. This is by no means the only lesson from losing a loved one.

I remember the day after my brother's death talking with his wife Betty and saying. "You know Betty, God must have something very important for Steve to do." Betty turned to me and said: "Can't you see he has done it already." I asked her what she meant and she said "Do you know how many lives your brother's death has effected? If God had something special for Steve to do, he has already done it." Now that was faith that I was unaware at the time existed. As I look back at that situation and see what happened after that I truly can say God works in amazing ways. You see during my brother's illness he was sent to a research hospital in Texas. It was there that Arthur a Catholic priest had first met my brother and his wife. Betty was a woman who had amazing faith, which I am sure this priest came to realize. No one, not even my sister-in-law Betty, would have imagined that she would eventually go on to marry a priest who was visiting my brother while he was sick in the hospital. After my brother died Arthur felt as though the children needed a father. Even though he had been a Catholic priest for more than twenty years, he requested that he be allowed to leave the priesthood he was told no. Yet he listened to the voice of God within and became a husband and father to my brother's wife and children. They have been incredibly happy for more than twenty years now. This man Arthur was able to hear God speaking with him and understood the freedom that Jesus was trying to teach.

If we look at how Jesus taught us to speak and listen to our Creator, who is a part of our own essence, then we will understand a little better that God loves us unconditionally. This is because we are His. Unfortunately, humankind's desire to control other human beings has corrupted that creative genius, which is God and a part of our normal everyday life.

What a different world this would be if each one of us knew in our soul that we are God's creation. How many of us know and believe that each time we make a decision we express the creative essence of God. If we did then we would understand what Jesus was trying to say.

CHAPTER 6
LOVE AND FORGIVENESS

If you can, imagine riding in an automobile and traveling towards the South Pole. Once we reach the South Pole and cross it, we begin traveling north towards the North Pole of the earth. Once we reach the North Pole and cross over it, we are again traveling south. But if we are in the same automobile and traveling east on the equator then we may travel east for eternity and never come to west. And if we started out travelling west, we could travel west for eternity and never run into East. So, the Bible tells us that God puts our transgressions, as far is the east from the west, this means that they are out of sight, out of mind (Psalms 103:12). God knows that we sometimes do not choose the choice of His will, but the experience is still important. This is the free will and creativity inherent in our essence, which is God.

I remember one time sitting in a group where a man was talking about how bad he was. I immediately was given an urging from within to say to this man that there are none of us who are bad. We just have made a choice that was not good. Can we be Sons/Daughters of God and be bad? Never. We must separate the behavior from who we are. I cannot emphasize enough that to understand God we must understand how He talks to us. This is not always easy to explain in a word, that is why parables are so important.

George Fox. the founder of the Society of Friends (Quakers) knew the scriptures very well, while he was on a pilgrimage for four years, he almost gave up hope in understanding the deeper essence of life. When he had come to wit's end and could find no man that would give him the peace he was seeking, and life had somehow lost its meaning, then behold, that of God which he termed "the light within", spoke to him and said:

> *"There is One, even Christ Jesus, that can speak to thy condition. And when I heard it, my heart did leap for joy."* [1]

This was the beginning of the Society of Friends. It is the very core of Fox's belief that within each man there is "that of God, or the Spirit of the Divine." As Jesus, Fox believed that our life here and now was especially important. For the last 300 years Quakers have been as much concerned about social justice, as Jesus was two thousand years ago. If we as Children of God could see "that of God within" every human being, then we could transcend the stereotypical burden of religious institutions and live the spiritual life. As stated below, so many people throughout the ages have spoken messages of truth. Even after the Bible was written I am convinced that others were able to listen and understand the languages of the soul. This is proof that God is still speaking, listening and inspiring those who know His language. It is hard to accept and believe that truth can only come from someone who professes to be a religious affiliate of some denomination.

> *"For my thoughts are not your thoughts, neither are your ways my ways saith the lord. For as the heavens are higher than the earth, so are my ways higher than your ways, and my thoughts titan your thoughts"* (Isaiah. 55: 8-9).

An experience of mine, which I have come to realize, was God speaking directly to me happened one day while fishing. I was out in the ocean on a boat with my friend Mike. We were way out, and you could see no land in any direction you looked. We were trolling for Sailfish and I was at the front of the boat dozing somewhere in between being awake and asleep but in my mind, I remember thinking about God, and believing that if God heard my thoughts, we would catch a fish. All of a sudden, the fishing reel started singing as a big sailfish was on the line, and at that moment, when I came to consciousness or became fully awake, the thought came to my mind and said, "I have just let you know that I exist and answered your thought." This, I am sure, was soul talk.

One of the many personal experiences that I have gone through, has made me aware of how religion has created separateness. A man whom I had come to know through my management of a service station in Florida, whose name was Emerys, said to me, "John, I do not understand why you are not prejudiced towards me a black man? You always treat me like a brother." My response to Emery was "I treat people as they treat me, we are all the same color on the inside." It was years later that I began to see what real racism, prejudice, injustice and being on the other side of society's fences really means. Even so, as I reflect on my answer to Emery's question. I see the fallacy in my thinking. It should not depend on how others treat us; we should always try and look above the circumstance and treat all people with respect even if they do not treat us properly. I did not see or know the God that dwells within us all at that time.

I think this is the real genius of Jesus. He was able to see above the behavior of another human being even if it was against him. This does not mean that we should be silent if we see something that is wrong. Gandhi was clear about that and used his example of non-violent resistance or civil disobedience. Striking back is a reaction that based on the laws of physics or the physical world will always result or can be expected to get a reaction in return. For every action there is a reaction, but the Godly laws operate differently. The spiritual law of Jesus was that of forgiveness. Yet, forgiveness when we have wronged another or even ourselves, is such a powerful force we rarely can imagine its effect. Those who are forgiven much, love much. To whom much is given, much is required (Luke 12:48). When we have been blessed by God and understand His guiding us through spiritual awareness, we are only too happy to do that which is asked of us. This is beyond most people's ability to understand because they are unable to operate from God's point of view.

Each day living in prison makes a person realize their Invisibility to a soul connection. In contrast, visibility becomes a handicap when someone does something wrong whether inside the walls or outside. Every day as men walk through the halls of prison, there is a sense of tension. This sense is always looming as a presence. Invisibility makes one feel as though they do not exist. At one time this writer was told, be courteous to those in authority and greet them with respect. Today both convicts and prison employees do not respect one another as living breathing human beings, but as invisible entitles that have no value unless something is needed or there is the opportunity to reprimand.[2]

Very often while walking through the halls of prison, a person may revert back to his upbringing not thinking about the present place of confinement. It is a major accomplishment to keep oneself from being hardened and callous in everyday prison life. Many times, I will say good day, hello, or how are you to an inmate, civilian or guard just as a normal habit, of being a social person that sees worth and being alive among God's creation. It is a stark awakening to be completely ignored as the invisibility is brought to the forefront. So many times, I want to say to myself, "Don't waste your breath on speaking to anybody but those you know." Yet in actuality that is also an awakening. Many times throughout the daily prison experience people are dealing with problems. They may be as simple as not having any money in the commissary, no cigarettes. Then again it may be something as serious as the dying of a person close to the heart with no ability to be present at the funeral. Daily struggles involving family, friends, and lovers add to the hopeless state of being invisible to oneself. No longer being able to deal with the simple but important interactions between other human beings, invisibility has a detrimental effect on one's psyche. However, the shroud of invisibility can disappear, and the aura of reality comes speeding to consciousness very quickly. This can happen when another convict, civilian or guard, sees you do something wrong. The same officer that you may have said hello to 100 times and never responded is now demanding an answer and your attention. This is a phenomenon that goes on across the board. A convict, who has never spoken with you even though you have said good morning or hello many times, is now upset because you stepped on his toe or were on the phone when he needed to use it. Now you are no longer invisible but recognized in this lonely existence. I say lonely because although there are hundreds of people around you each day there is little contact or conversation between men. Maybe a hitting of knuckles or some other jailhouse gesture to signify recognition and some type of connective-ness, but that is the exception not the rule. This invisibility has left a person like me realizing that in prison we must constantly work on looking within ourselves for that sense of self and importance that we possess. After many years in prison the psychological effect of invisibility takes its toll, and someone preparing for release must be counseled in this area, otherwise the overwhelming sense of being invisible when released can cause a false sense of friendship and understanding with people we meet. For many having had no responsibility behind the wall, it is difficult to suddenly be faced with decision-making tasks. Asking others for help who seem friendly can be a trap. Most prisoners when first released are starved for social interaction. Prison makes most people have a feeling of insecurity, and the walk back to a sense of self is a long slow walk towards visibility.

We see life as a problem until we reach a point of inner peace and then we begin to understand that this existence is a fleeting moment in time. Stumbling blocks are nothing more than steppingstones on the journey to knowing who we are. We must come to understand and embrace our sense of Spiritual being-ness not just our human experiences. This is an attitude we must embrace if we are to see what is important. If we were to live today as if it were our last in this world, we would live much differently.

> *"The more one forgets himself- by giving himself to a cause to serve or another person to love - the more human."*

This kind of talk, which the so-called wise and understanding of this world regard as madness, calls all human beings together to share a soul experience. This is no easy challenge. It takes courage and the belief that we are all incredibly special and of equal value through soul connections. The religion of the soul is universal love for all humankind.

> *"For consider your call, brethren; not many of you were wise according to worldly standards, not many powerful, not many were of noble birth; but God chose what is foolish in the world to shame the wise, God chose what is weak in the world to shame the strong, God*

chose what is low and despised in the world, even things that are not, to bring to nothing things that are, so that no human being might boast in the presence of God." (1 Corinthians. 1:26)

This soul existence is manifest in our creative essence, that of God within and is explained simply but profoundly in a book by Ishmael Garcia, *Dignidad* (Dignity) where he states;

"The vision of the Kingdom that is at the center of Jesus' message and ministry motivates Hispanics and gives us hope for the possibilities of a better future within history, and perseverance in the struggle for the creation of a more humane world. It frees us to become creative agents because we are assured that God will consummate His purpose of new and abundant life for humanity and that all we create, which fits within God's loving and just design, will endure the perils of time. When the Kingdom is at the center of our life, we do not need to make one of our lessor creations the center of meaning. Nor do we need to oppress and dominate others to feel secure and in control. On the contrary, we are prone to take the risk of opening ourselves to those who are different and include those who are not like us within our sphere of life-giving love. We are also made free to be authentic and affirm the uniqueness of our being, and the uniqueness of those who are different from us."

This statement above reinforces my own belief that Jesus was trying to teach us to understand our own creativity and to use it. If every person understood their spiritual connection to one another, they would stand up for what is right no matter what the consequences. Can you imagine if millions of people decided they had enough of dominant society's oppression?

If we lived this way, we would be living the religion of the soul, and there would be peace in the whole world. In many instances we no longer allow ourselves to be open to the groaning and direction of our spiritual guide within. Religion cannot solve the ills of our society until we embrace the teaching of all those who seek truth, that of God within. This requires our belief that we are gods, and our ability to understand the languages of the soul (Luke 17: 21). When we realize who we are and walk a life of truth and love we become a living Bible to all that hear and see us.

In George Fox's journal we have a description of what the awakening and realization of what Fox meant in his own words.

> *"The lord hath opened to me by His invisible power how that every man was enlightened by the divine light of Christ; and I saw it shine through all and that they believed on it came out of condemnation and came to the light of life and became the children of it; but they that hated it and did not believe in it though they made a profession of Christ. This I saw in the pure openings of the light without the help of any man, neither did I then know where to find it. For I saw in that light the Spirit which was before scripture was given forth, that all must come to that*

> *spirit- if they would know God or Christ or die scriptures aright—which they that gave them forth were led and taught by."*

In this very passage. Fox has clearly set forth the specific chapters of John 15:13 regarding the Spirit of God available to us all:

> *"Howbeit when He, the Spirit of truth is come he will guide you into all truth; for he shall not speak of himself but whatsoever he shall hear, that shall he speak, and he will show you things to come."*

This is hard to accept after being told for a lifetime that we are sinners and unworthy of God's unconditional love. My own recent life experience of God talking to me directly has made me realize and understand soul talk.

Our highest understanding of who we are and who God is can be known by our experience of joy, truth, and love through spiritual experiences. This is why the parables of Jesus are so important. It gives us a clear picture of the feeling and the experience as well as what people thought before they even asked Jesus to do something. Jesus gave us a picture in words of the human condition. The life of the soul.

Think of the woman in the Bible story who had been bleeding for twelve years. As Jesus and the disciples were going to the rabbi's home, a woman who had been sick for twelve years with internal bleeding came up behind Him and touched a tassel of His robe, for she thought. "If I only touch Him. I will be healed." Jesus turned around **(Knowing that power went out of Him) and** spoke to her,

> *"Daughter," He said, "all is well Your Faith has healed you".*

And the woman was well from that moment. The healing power of the Spirit came from the bosom of the creative force within this woman, and she was healed. This is a perfect example of Jesus understanding that she was a daughter of God. A child of God

> *"The wind bloweth where it listeneth and thou hearest the sound thereof, but canst not tell whence it cometh, and whither it goeth: so is every one that is born of the spirit" (John 3: 8-9).*

Knowing how we can talk with God and how he talks with us is a revelation that comes to us when we understand and recognize our spiritual essence. Each day it is important for us to live in the moment and to create our understanding of self, which is spiritual wellbeing.

As I look back on my own childhood and the society of modern-day America, religions are steeped in an atmosphere of separateness, which is in contrast to God's teaching. This is exactly what Jesus was trying to expose. Jesus had no intention of beginning a religion but was concerned with the condition of humankind in society, and the ability to rise above the circumstances of life in an alternative spiritual transcendence. This is our challenge, to live the spiritual life in the here and now. Can you imagine If 1 million people in New York City came together and demanded equal housing using non-violent methods, like everybody sleeping in front of City Hall? Gandhi had everybody walk to the sea for salt instead of paying the tax on salt. Godly ways of love can overcome evil. I find it amazing to think of how much God loves us. If we were able to define or express what God "is," we would invariably use the words love and truth. These words portray a picture in our minds of a connection between

God and creation, God the spirit and our spiritual self.

I remember one time when I lived in Florida and on my way home from work late in the afternoon it had been raining for several hours. As I approached the ramp to the expressway, I noticed two young men walking with knapsacks on their backs. I stopped the car and asked them if they needed a ride. They said, "yes". As we drove south towards my home in Deerfield Beach. I asked them where they were going. They said they were on their way to Key West, which was at least 75 miles away. It was already beginning to get dark as we reached the exit, so I asked them if they had a place to sleep for the night. They said they would be sleeping at a park in Ft. Lauderdale. I said to them, it looks, as though it will rain all night, are you sure? I offered them a place to sleep at my home and a bite to eat. Understandably, they seemed apprehensive. Little did they know that I was also concerned. I wasn't sure how my wife Bonnie would react, to me bringing two strangers home for the night. Anyway, when I walked in the door and said that I had brought two young men home so they could get out of the rain. Bonnie wasn't happy. She asked me if I was crazy, not knowing who these kids were. After a short time of talking, these two young men and my wife seemed more at ease. Bonnie then offered them some dry clothes to wear while theirs were in the dryer. We added a few potatoes to the meal, and all ate. My wife put some blankets on the living room floor and after talking until it was late, we all went to sleep. The next morning it was still raining, and the street was quite flooded. I went to work and about 9:30 in the morning the rain stopped, and we had a terribly busy day replacing many mufflers that people had lost due to the rain. On my way home I was reflecting on the day's happenings. I really did not think we would have any business that day. I was wrong. Anyway, when I got home my wife had a smile and a look of pure joy upon her face which I could not understand. Before I could even ask her what was happening, she gave me a big hug and said I really am glad you brought those kids home last night. I was surprised by what she said. Then she told me that when they all woke up that morning our children and these two young men had played, talked and ate breakfast. The boys told my wife that they were scared the night before because they did not know who I was and why I was being nice to them. Sometime around 4 o'clock in the afternoon my wife took the two young men to the entrance of the expressway, hugged each one of them, gave them a small pocket Bible, and said goodbye. There was a big rainbow in the sky. On the way home, my wife passed the house, of our gardener and thought to herself. I really hope our gardener brings us some of those delicious grapefruits soon. When my wife arrived home sitting up against the front door of the house was a big bag of grapefruit. She told me she cried and realized that God is always working. We all can help others by making the right choice.

> *"You are the light of the world... No one after lighting a lamp puts it under a bushel basket, but on a lampstand, and it gives light to all in the house. In the same way, let your light shine before others, so that they may see your good works and give glory to your Father in heaven"*
> *(Matthew 5:14-16).*

If we were to look back on the first century church, we would see a true fellowship of Jesus' followers as an example of soul connections.

> *"And all that believed were together and had all things common; And sold their possessions and goods, and parted them*

> *to all persons, as every person had need.*
> *And they are continuing daily with one*
> *accord in the temple, and breaking bread*
> *from house to house, did eat their meat*
> *with gladness and singleness of heart,*
> *Praising God, and having favor with all the*
> *people. And the Lord added to the church*
> *daily such as should be saved"*
> *(Acts 2: 44-47).*

Only in the last three years, after attending New York Theological Seminary, have I begun to understand what many of the Bible's teachings really mean that the "church" from Jesus' perspective (the body of Christ) are those who follow Him. The Church as Jesus explained churches are not physical structures where people meet, but literally means "those who are called out". We have not followed Jesus' Teaching but instead have become pawns of religious institutions and physical structures we call the church, which Jesus despised. Unfortunately. Christianity falls within this spectrum. Christianity cannot deal with the issues of life because we look not into each human being's heart, but rather at our physical differences. We don't look at the root of crime, but we build prisons. Christianity and other religions respond to worldly events by preaching the hereafter and personal salvation instead of responsibility for our brothers and sisters as connected through the soul experience here and now. If we really believe we are God's, then we are connected to each other. Until we accept who we are and the responsibility of that burden, we are lost. The parables spoke to humankind's condition, crossing all social, political, and cultural barriers, transcending the physical form looking deep within to the spiritual experience.

Jesus said,

"I leave you peace, not the peace of this world but my peace, do not be troubled. I have overcome this world" (John 14:27).

Most of us have forgotten how incredibly special we are. I remember in fourth grade I had an English teacher named Mrs. Beam. She was very dedicated to making sure we knew who we were. Just recently as I was sitting down gazing out the window over the Hudson river one of the poems that she made us memorize came to mind and is a clear expression of how incredibly special we are.

That poem goes as follows:

TREES

By Joyce Kilmer

I think that I shall never see
a poem as lovely as a tree
A tree whose hungry mouth is pressed against
the Earth's sweet flowing breast.

A tree that may in summer wear
a nest of Robin's in her hair
Poems are made by fools like me
but only God can make a tree.

If a tree can only be made by God how marvelous is the creation of humankind? Almost every morning I sit and look upon the wonder of creation from my window, even though in prison. A quiet time of solitude and awe at the awesome creation unfolding before me. Several months ago, as I sat looking out the window the following words came to me.

HUDSON RIVER VIEW

AWESOME SIGHTS
BEHOLD THE SKY
OF COLORS SWARMING
ACROSS THE EYE.

OF BEAUTY BEHOLDEN
TO GOD ON HIGH
OF MAJESTY'S PATIENCE
AMONGST THE CRY.

OF WRETCHED WAR
OF DEATH FOR NIGH
LACK OF SOUL CONNECTIONS.

WHY?

I am so thankful that God has given us gifts for sharing His thoughts and that we are able to listen and speak with Him.

CHAPTER 7
THE CREATOR

*"To some God and Jesus may appeal in a
way other than to us: some may come to
faith in God and to love, without a
conscious attachment to Jesus. Both
Nature and good men besides Jesus may
lead us to God. They who seek God with
all their hearts must, however, some day
on their way meet Jesus."*[1]

The quote, which seems fitting in the context, in which I
am speaking is a realization of the dynamism of Jesus and the
truth he shared. Clearly Jesus' teaching and His ability to rise
above the circumstances of oppression as a person with "His
back to the wall," speaks loudly to our own circumstances
today. Keeping in mind Jesus as a historical figure couched as
a man and the Divine figure as Son of God is instructive.

Two thousand years after the death of Jesus, many people
are still trying to understand who Jesus was and know who we
are. For many of us our communication with God began when
we were young. Our parents, teachers, religious leaders, and
others told us that when we made a wrong choice that we
were bad and could expect punishment. How can we as
children of the Divine be bad? It is our behavior that is bad.
We never separated our behavior from who we are because
of what we were told.

Therefore, we need to understand and believe that we are
God's children and that we have forgotten or never learned
how to listen and understand God's language. I do not want

to sound other worldly, but in most cases, we are raised being told that we are sinners and separated from God, not children of God. This is difficult to overcome, and in many cases takes us a whole lifetime to realize. For some, it is never realized. This I believe was what Jesus' message was all about. Letting us know that we are children of God and understanding His languages. Jesus taught us a way of life and gave us an experiential method of realizing who we are. That is why the parables are so important. Jesus was able to use nature and other world spiritual power to paint a picture different from the "conventional wisdom of His day".[2]

Jesus was a radical, turning His world upside down.[3] This is where I think we must understand what Jesus was trying to say. He said concerning the Last Supper "Do this in memory of me." Today across the world when offering communion, the celebrant says, "The Body of Christ" and we say "Amen", affirming our belief in the Divinity of Jesus. He did not say that he had come to start another religion. He was really trying to make people understand that they were God's creation and that they needed to remember that they are made in His image. Therefore if "Ye are gods" or Children of God we should live life abundantly" (John 10:10). Therefore share a supper with me to remember what I am trying to tell you. This is my body, which I have given up for you.

> *"All who listen to my instructions and follow them are wise, like a man who builds his house on solid rock. Though the rain comes in torrents, and the floods rise, and the storm winds beat against his house, it won't collapse, for it is built on rock. But those who hear my instructions and ignore them are foolish, like a man who builds his house on sand. For when*

the rains and floods come, and storm winds beat against his house, it will fall with a mighty crash" (Matthew. 7:24).

It is my opinion that the real hope of our human existence is to live a life that cannot be robbed of the Godly spirit and the creative integrity we all possess. Bill Weber clearly stated in his book, *Led by the Spirit* [4] how our creative genius inherent within us all as Children of God can be expressed when we trust and understand communication from and with God.

Howard Thurman has said for those of us who find ourselves with "our backs to the wall"[5] we must overcome that which tries to kill the knowledge and memory of God's spirit within. Nothing can kill the essence of God within, but we can allow ourselves to be so overwhelmed and overburdened with a feeling of hopelessness that we can forget that the spiritual world exists and that we are God's Son's/Daughters. Nothing can hurt that which is ineffable. The prison experience is how I became aware of our ability to rise above the situation we are in or put the spirit to sleep. Additionally, no matter what circumstance we find ourselves living, we can look deep within and see the reality of who we are. We do not have to be in prison or suffer a tragedy to understand God's talking with us. [We call these aspects of God other names such as inner beauty or universalness of existence, in lieu of Inner Light, Holy Spirit, or that of God in each of us, the Divine spark, Atman, or enlightenment, etc. etc. Yet all these names are symbols, for that which we can only remember by understanding God talking to us through experience, thought, and creative integrity based in love and compassion which are touchstones of the spirit...] Meditation, prayer, silent worship, can be synonymous with our own personal conversation and relationship with God, but how many of us attune to God's language which is spiritually spoken?

For many of these reasons, my personal attachment to Quakerism has grown, because that which I do not understand, is understandable from within. If we can escape from the guilt of religion, concerned so much with sin and guilt, we may very well be free of our burdens. The amazing part of the Gospels and Jesus' teaching was the ability to forgive oneself for our human weakness. We cannot see the wind, love, peace, or what touches the inner part of our heart, but we know they exist. When we look at a painting or hear music it touches a deep part of our being, that of our spiritual essence, that of God. Here is an example of Jesus' ability to know and show that He was the Son of God and that those with Him had the same ability. If God is One then we are all children of God and since God is Spirit, there are no differences in His eyes. God does not see color, race, religion, poor, rich, etc. He sees all of us as children first, then our choices and the circumstances we find ourselves to be in. This did not come without a price, for God gave up the power to control us. He gave us free will and creativity which is His essence and ours.

Gustavo Guiterriz in his Book, *On Job,* clearly states that God is a weak God. But this is not the weakness from a human perspective but from God's willingness to allow us the ability to choose. Therefore, God is a God of unity. Unfortunately, it is man's religion that has caused us to see with jaded eyes humanity in the physical form instead of seeing with a God's eye vision that which is spirit and our own Godliness. For many years I was under the impression that if we did good. God would reward us. This retributive belief in God is the normal way of thinking for most people. We are conditioned from an early age that if we are good, good will come to us. Therefore, many of us become people pleasers, believing that whatever we do in this world will be rewarded. This concept is narrow in thinking and puts God into a pigeonhole mentality. If this were so, then we would take away God's omniscience. As the parable says. The Sun shines on both good and bad. This was explained well in the parable about the tares and the wheat where they grow together and are separated in the end. We must realize that God does not look or judge our actions from a human perspective, therefore we cannot try to understand God's justice. This is where faith and the realization that God loves us must be embraced. It is His gratuitiveness that controls. Grace is not grace if we believe it can be bought. It is my opinion that Jesus showed us a way of life that allows outside experience to melt away from that which he called the "Kingdom of God within" which is a sacred and indestructible essence. It is the spiritual experience that is God talking to us.

Strangely, for me this realization has come about, in a unique yet powerful awakening. Had someone told me that I would one day embrace the teachings of a man named George Fox and the Society of Friends I would have told them that they were wrong. Likewise, had someone said that I would serve a considerable amount of my life in prison for killing two people I would have also said they were wrong. I could not kill anybody. So, I thought. Yet it is my belief and spiritual conviction that because of these occurrences I now know that I embellish the spirit within and have come to know a shadow of the divine through this experience. Many people who are physically free, are imprisoned and many imprisoned, are free and at peace.

It may be a pleasant experience to hear a man or woman preaching from the pulpit about God's salvation plan for the hereafter, but Jesus was also concerned about the here and now. Can we believe that God is only concerned with saving souls but does not care about the oppressed, marginalized, the poor, etc. etc.? This is not the kind of God that I want to follow. Jesus is the perfect example of what we should be about. In His walk on this Earth, Jesus talked about doing His Father's business and man persecuted Him for that.

In *Joshua,* by Joseph F. Girzone, the author allows us to see how Joshua is thinking. A character named Aaron asks Joshua;

"How did you become the way you are? Who taught you all the things you believe in?" His answer was, "I experience what I believe, so I know what I believe is true". Aaron says, what do you mean? Joshua's answer is instructive for all of us,

> *"Each person looks at life through a different vision. Three men look at a tree. One man will see so many board feet of valuable lumber worth so much money. The second man will see it as so much firewood to be burned, to keep his family warm in the winter. The third man will see it as a masterpiece of God's creative art, given to man as an expression of God's love and enduring strength, with a value far beyond its worth in money and firewood. What we live for determines what we see in life and gives clear focus to our inner vision."*

The Bible may teach us to have reverence for those in power but I am a firm believer that when we see wrong, we must speak out against wrong otherwise we have sold our integrity for that which has no value. When will we wake up to the call of Jesus and be able to answer "Yes, I am here no matter what, the consequences?" Jesus by example and parable made that perfectly clear. It is unfortunate that religion, including Christianity has created separateness between that of God (the Kingdom within) and human beings. The genius of Jesus is His integrity grounded in love knowing full well that the Kingdom of God is within each of us.

Jesus knew from a human experience that there would always be those outside the mainstream of society. He Himself was outside and refused to sell His soul to be made King. In this sense I believe that Jesus was able to find a way of relating to all humankind in His statement to those who heard Him.

> *"Then Jesus got into a boat and started across the lake with His disciples. Suddenly a terrible storm came up, with waves higher than the boat. But Jesus was asleep. The disciples went to Him and wakened Him, shouting "Lord, save us we are sinking!" But Jesus answered, "Oh you men of little faith. Why are you so frightened?" Then he stood up and rebuked the wind and waves, and the storm subsided, and all was calm. The disciples just sat there, awed! "Who is this they asked themselves, that even the winds and the sea obey Him?"* (Matthew 8:27).

Jesus tells us we will do and see greater things than this, if we only have faith as big as a mustard seed. We have become so brainwashed with what people have told us or what our parents say or what the preacher says that we no longer know how to listen to what God says. How could God be a punishing God when he created us in His image? He loves us. How could Jesus say the above if those with him were afraid? The reason is they did not know who they were. Children of the Creator.

Why then are there so many who are poor and treated unjustly? Let's be realistic and not find someone or something to blame. Let's take responsibility and admit that we as human beings are responsible for the world as it is today because we do not listen or know when God is speaking to us. God gave us the ability to create and choose and He will not interfere in that aspect of His creation. Jesus gave us the answer: "His yoke is easy." Many times, we go through tribulations for others to see our behavior, but God is there to carry us if we struggle. God will never put us through more than we can bear. But how many of us listen to what Jesus is saying? We continue to follow religious leaders who apply the law rigidly instead of remembering that we are gods and therefore can have a continuing communication with the Creator by knowing how we can talk to Him. This may be too hard for some to accept and or believe and they will continue to wallow in their own guilt, and fear created by man. Love and hate are the two great opposites. The ends of the universe, positive and negative. Whatever we call the opposites.

If we believe that our Maker (Father/Mother) (The Creator of all),

> *"Formed (humankind) from the dust of the ground, and breathed into (humankind's) nostrils the breath of life', and humankind became a living soul."* (Genesis 2: 7).

Then, we understand we are creativity manifest in the physical realm. The above biblical quote may be viewed as reality or a symbolic expression of the creation of humankind that could be understood from a human perspective. Therefore, if we were to consider the above statements, as true, it is much easier for us to understand who we are, knowing that we are the essence of the Creator. We are not the Creator of all, but nonetheless we are gods. As a result, there is an especially important connection and commonality between the Creator and each one of us.

Thomas Aquinas', in his *Sumnia Theologize,* stated:

> *"We cannot know what God is but only what God is not."*

Conversely then. I would venture to say, that God cannot know what God is physically, unless God knows what God is not physically, therefore humankind.

I am quite sure that someone will argue God knows everything therefore He did not need to create humankind to understand the physical manifestation. I would both agree and disagree in that God is spirit and until that spirit becomes physical it did not exist. Who am I to question what God does? The spiritual manifestation of God in the physical realm is the miracle of life itself and a gift from God. Is this so hard to believe when Jesus claimed to be the Son of God? Do we believe that the Creator of the entire universe cannot appear in physical form? Opposites. The power of choice. Physical vs. spiritual. This is another connection that allows us to understand our connection to the Divine.

Whatever we think of Buddha. Mohammed. Gandhi. Mother Theresa. Ruth, Mary Magdalene, George Fox, Malcolm X. Martin Luther King, Jr., and all others who have searched for "truth," is of course important. And I believe that every one of these men and women were messenger angels that spoke God's language. However, what is more important is our search and the finding of a personal relationship with our inner spirit by embracing the essence of the Divine within and sharing our experience of "truth." For then, not only will we have found who we are, but we will also begin to understand what we are called to do on this plane of existence. This is what we must consider, for no religion or manmade institution has a monopoly on the Creator of all, the "I Am."

In an interesting article by Jan Arriens, *The Place of Jesus in Quaker Universalism,* a noted point of conflict in institutional Christianity is brought up for review. Many of the problems associated with reading the scripture are caused by not using a realistic and common-sense approach. We rarely keep in mind that we are Sons/Daughters of God.

Jesus said,

> *"No Man Cometh to the Father but by Me"*
> (John 14:6).

This has no doubt been a source of considerable trouble for those who defend the Christian religion and even those who see this as exclusivity. Yet, looking at this from a school of thought based on Eastern philosophy and enlightenment it is easily understood. How could God who is the mother/father of all human beings operate with exclusivity?

When Jesus said, *"I am the way, the truth, and the life; no man cometh to the Father but by me"(John 14:6),* I believe Jesus was trying to explain that following Him required the realization that, "that which dwells within humankind is the true essence of God." Our ability for overcoming the world is in my words and parables and you will find "The Way, The Truth, and the Life." This is only one example of the genius of Jesus and the use of parables. Therefore the "God-spells (Gospels) which continuously portray a roadmap experienced in the circumstance that Jesus found himself are illustrative. Yet the parables and what Jesus experienced are applicable today. The human condition with all its technological breakthroughs still fails to address the most important aspect of being human, the condition of the soul. The inner being and humankind's search for meaning in life. When Jesus tells a learned man that he must be born again, He is trying to make Nicodemus understand that the spiritual essence within must come alive. To understand Jesus as a man is noble, but to think that this came from intellectual prowess is ridiculous. Read the parables, they cannot be learned from academic teaching. If Jesus was not the physical manifestation of God, then God does not exist. How did He learn all of this? Is it impossible for God to experience the human condition? Of course not. Jesus knew He was God. If Jesus did not know who He was or where He came from or where He was going. He was the greatest lunatic of all time.

In our world today we see many people who are dissatisfied with religious institutions. More and more people are looking within themselves to understand who they are. Even the person who decides and says he believes in <u>nothing</u>, must admit that "the nothing decision"; "The thought", becomes something. What is that? Logic? The reasoning minds? The Creator expressed? Intelligence? Truth? Vibration? Is it the study of God's spirit manifest in man, Logos-ology? I am not attempting to prove that God exists with such a simple explanation, only raise the thought for reflection. Proving the existence of God scientifically is impossible. We cannot see the Spirit of God, but like the wind we cannot see, we can experience it.

Pascal once said:

"The heart has its reasons of which reason knows nothing."

The noted theologian Gustavo Gutierrez in his book. *On Job, (God-Talk, Suffering of the innocent)*, starts off with the comment that "Theology is talk about God." I believe there is more. Theology is much more than just talk about God, but it is also talk with God. For talk about God and humankind is really talk about the communication between God and humankind. Therefore, theology would seem to encompass the study of **communication** between humankind and the Creator.

CHAPTER 8
SOULSHIP

"Reason must develop into intuition, knowledge must expand into wisdom, and mere feeling must give place to love. We must listen less to the voices around us, and more to the still small voice that speaks within." [1]

We all find our own understanding of self in different experiences. For me, the tragic results of my behavior have been prison. The past thirteen years have afforded me the opportunity to look back at my past in an honest search of my pattern of behavior and of who I was and who I am today. Having done a genuine and sincere evaluation of my past, the following comes to mind. I realize that emotions played a major role in my inability to control my actions. One of the most important lessons I have learned while in prison is that "Emotions are poor masters but good servants". This is just one of the languages of the soul where God talks to us. I was not listening. Had I learned or known that God was speaking to me in His language years ago I would not have been trying to mask my feelings with the use of alcohol and prescription drugs. Prison forced and afforded me the opportunity to look within and see the person I never knew. As I grew to understand myself better, I was able to purge myself of poor attitudes and behavior. In prison I began to see that while in society I did not conform to community standards which my dad had long tried to show me. This acceptance of authority and owning of responsibility for my actions began a process of growth. This allowed me to atone for what I had done and strive to be a better person in the future. I needed to become more in tune with my own feelings. I needed to know my own soul experience. This enabled me to grow both emotionally and spiritually, while understanding the feelings and needs of others. With the help of trained, caring professionals I understood the devastating effects that substance abuse had played in my life. Without the use of drugs to mask my feelings I encountered a painful process but one of abundant awakening. I began slowly seeking the strength of that which was greater than I, and eventually came to a relationship with a God who had been on the outside of my life instead of being a part of my life.

As part of the Nassau County DART program, I began to find a spirituality that was long masked using drugs. Eventually I would become the facilitator of this special program and lead 42 men in prayer and thanksgiving daily. Under the direction of Bobby Moore, a wounded healer who initiated the program, I began to hear God speaking to my soul. I will never forget what happened one morning as I was sitting at the breakfast table with fellow prisoners. An officer walked up to the table and picked up the spoon in the bowl of prunes and dumped a spoonful on top of my French toast. He then made the comment while laughing that he thought I needed some prunes. As a result, I felt myself getting upset, so instead I just got up and went to my cube and opened the Bible and started to read. Several hours later a young man who had been sitting across from me came to my cube and asked if I was alright. I told him I was fine. I had learned a lesson early on from a remarkable man that worked for the Town of Hempstead's alcoholic program. Once a week as part of the DART program Peter Messina, a psychologist would come to the jail and talk with the men in a group therapy session. On one occasion I asked him some questions about how to control anger. His statement was an especially important lesson. Peter taught me that whatever anybody else does is their responsibility, whatever we do is our response - ability. This little lesson which I had put into practice saved me from causing myself further problems. The interesting part of this story is after this problem with the officer he was not at work for the next six weeks. When he did come back to work, he came to me and apologized telling me that he had been in a rehabilitation center for alcoholism and admitted that on the morning in question he had been drunk. This is just one experience that we all need to learn and was a further realization and impetus to search for knowledge.

As a result, I became involved with almost any program offered for self-improvement. I became quite aware of the prison atmosphere and had to adjust to the surroundings. On more than one occasion I had to make the choice between going to church or having my radio and commissary purchases stolen. I wanted to learn more about how God was guiding my life so I chose church. Although I didn't know it then I was beginning to understand the languages of the soul. God was talking with me.

These programs, caring people and my own will to change has allowed me to minister to others in many gratifying ways. My life is no longer that which is what I need, but the understanding that many are worse off than I. Today I am the person who I want to be, I cannot change yesterday although I would like to be able to do so. Today and in the future there is clearly fertile ground for my ability to help others and continue to speak with God.

Editor James Melvin Washington writes in his introduction of *Two Centuries of Prayers by African Americans,*

> *"Prayer is an attempt to count the stars of the soul. Under its sacred canopy, an oratory of hope echoes the vast immediate distances of who we are and who we want to be."*

What I value most today is the gift from God, knowing who I am. As time has passed. I have overcome my feelings of inadequacy, loneliness, emotional powerlessness and matured. Through God I have come to know me, and have worked hard to strengthen my positive attributes, good qualities anti virtues while leaving behind the feeble and immature person I once was.

Many people talk about rehabilitation, but I believe that is not good enough. Rehabilitation only returns that which was defective to its original state, but transformation makes anew that which needs to be changed. This inner and outer transformation has been a gift. I can never pay the debt of those people's lives which have been forever lost.

How often today I speak with my daughter and ask her to take the time and smell a rose or look at the stars and see the beauty of the creation and understand who she is. A child of God.

My prayer today is that I may help others see life's beauty and its pitfalls. In this way I may be able to prevent others from the tragedy that I had to experience and the pain I have caused others along with the burden to society.

Having realized that God speaks with us and following that guidance, over the last 16 months I have successfully spearheaded a college project in the hopes of making our communities a safer place by allowing those in prison to further their education, even though this was eliminated by the government in 1995. Today this is a reality. It is my hope to continue with projects such as these whether I am incarcerated or released. I believe I have a duty to leave this world a better place, in an attempt to pay the debt I owe society and the community.

Pandita Ramabai an Indian sage said it differently, but it means the same thing:

> *"People must not only hear about the kingdom of God, but must see it in actual operation, on a small scale perhaps and in imperfect form, but a real demonstration nonetheless."*

When Jesus says:

> *"Come to me all whose burden is heavy, my yoke is light and I will give you rest"*
> (Matthew 11:30).

This is a way of overcoming the world. Those who are oppressed can be free. Over the last 40 years we have seen a tremendous surge in theological exegesis. Humankind has tried to understand God's purpose for living in this world and how we should apply those teachings. Liberation theology, black theology, feminist theology, etc., etc. Each one has tried to relate the God of then, too today's experience.

My own experience of prison is but another attempt to theologize God's word from a prison theological perspective. Hence prison theology. Yet this very attempt leads me to believe that although I profess to have something to say because of this prison experience, it is another example of separateness. True theological reflection must then be based on an experience unique to the individual from a journey within our own soul. God is much bigger than the different schools of thought, and human attempts to pigeonhole God may be part of the problem. In essence we begin to exhibit difference and forget God is One. That our experience is different than the next person's, is of course normal, as all human experience must be. Yet isn't God the one God of all? Is it time then that we see a Cosmos-theology that everybody fits into, with the search for truth as being most important? Was Jesus trying to say exactly that? That the road to God is a road that all who come to know God, can experience through Divine awakening. We have been asleep much too long. We have been taught that God is far away and that our personal relationship is based only on what we do, not on who we are. Who we are is one of the most important aspects of life that we will ever endeavor to understand? To be born of the Spirit has been thrown around for so long, but what does this term mean? The answer is quite simple; every parable that Jesus has given us leads us on that path to truth. Knowing that the spirit that dwells within us all must be born into our mind, and come to know that nothing, no matter how great or terrible, cannot destroy or hurt that which is not physical. That sounds simple yet when someone hurts our feelings, I would be the first to say that I am pained. Yet today I know that no matter what another person does can hurt, rob or destroy who I am a living-breathing child of God. Therefore, I am much bigger than what anybody can do to me if I know that in my heart and soul.

Jesus said follow me for my yoke is light and I will carry your burden. This is easy to say when we are comfortable and filled. Jesus' parables tell us that if we are really to know the spirit within and be reborn then we must concern ourselves with others whose yoke is heavy and have the faith and commitment to do the teaching that he has given us. Then and only then can we say I am your friend for I do what you have showed me to the least of these.

George Washington once said:

> *"Let us impart all the blessings we seek for ourselves to the whole family of humankind."*

It is my belief that the authentic community, which we are so much in need of today, must begin with the inner self. The spirituality and fellowship of true brethren is what we need to share. To be concerned about others and see the greater picture which binds us together. Then and only then can we be truly free. The following is my interpretation of what Jesus was trying to say in the context of understanding who we are and speaking and listening to God.

> *Dear Mom/Dad (Creator) thank you for loving me unconditionally and creating me.*
>
> *Dad/Mom. I know that you know, exactly what I need even before I ask you.*
>
> *May the joy you want for me be realized today. May I choose all experience according to your will and listen with my heart and soul to your guidance from within.*
>
> *I know that if I choose an experience not of your will, you will still love me, and I will learn from it.*
>
> *I thank you for allowing me to experience the choices I choose.*

May I live at peace with all those I meet each precious moment of life. May I choose love in all endeavors and be not afraid to create, forgive and remember who I am.

A child of God. I know you are with me this moment and forever, whether in spirit or in this body as I am a part of you. Amen.

I remember when I was first in the county jail in 1987, and I was listening to the radio a man commented that he had a PACT with God. **P** stands for praising God for all that he has given us each day. **A** is for admiring God for the greatness of His creation which includes me. **C** is for confessing to God that at times I have decided unwisely and that He still loves me. **T** is for thanking God for all that I am. I try and use this simple PACT each evening when I am going to bed. It is my reminder that God loves me, and that I am a child of the Divine. Therefore, an incredibly special expression of God's love.

If one person reads this book and finds a sense of peace, that of God within, or can recognize God speaking to them, I am thankful.

FOOTNOTES

INTRODUCTION:

1. <u>The Book of Embraces</u>, Eduardo Galleano.

2. The term God is used here to mean Creator and is not meant to be a cliché' for God, nor is it used to confine anyone's thoughts on a higher power.

3. Gustavo Gutierrez in his book <u>On Job</u> gives us a superb explanation of God's free and unmerited love, especially to the poor and forgotten and those who lack intellectual understanding. The babes of this world Intro, xii-xiii.

4. In a book written by Neale Donald Walsch, <u>Conversations with God,</u> Walsch mentions that feelings are the language of God. It is my belief that God talk is more varied than just feelings.

5. The concept of messenger angels was brought to my awareness by a Catholic Priest at Sing Sing Prison, Father Ronald Lemmert. On a Sunday morning it was the topic of his homily.

6. It is my belief that we need to talk with God, not to God.

7. <u>Guidepost Magazine</u>. Malcolm Muggeridge, March 1999.

8. This is a term which I believe is more in line with a belief in our commonality and more akin to the teachings of Jesus. The religion of the soul crosses all cultural and religious boundaries and any other barrier that humankind tries to erect.

9. I was first introduced to this thought by Sister Liu a Buddhist nun who is a volunteer here at Sing Sing Prison. Many of the New York State prisons have Buddhist centers. I first became aware of this through my friend Jack Madden who introduced me to Adrienne Simidian, a gentle spirit.

10. I use this term from my own understanding which transcends the common expectation of friend or wife in the particular case.

11. This is a term, which is used to identify the Society of Friends, established by George Fox in 1655. George Fox was a mystic believing that God talks with us when we are silent George Fox believed that as spiritually born individuals it is our responsibility to speak out against wrong. He spent many years in some of the worst prison conditions in England. Although the Quakers are seen as the first penitentiary builders in this country their sense of social justice and punishment was polluted. Therefore they refused to serve as members in the government because of their beliefs against violence and war. Today, Alternative to Violence projects (AVP) begun at Green Haven prison more than 30 years ago are practiced all over the world.

12. Many years ago while working in a service station as a mechanic an Italian gentleman and I were discussing our last names. His name was Fiore which means 'flowers'. Translated, Mandala means 'to search out'. The front cover illustration designed by Mr. Mandala, represents the circle of life and transcendence into another reality, that of the spiritual realm.

13. Jesus and the Disinherited, Howard Thurman. This term is used by Thurman and would seem to signify any and all who live a life of oppression, injustice, discrimination, and the plight of the masses in this world. All of the different kinds of suffering of humankind fall in this category.

14. An exceptionally good friend and graduate of New York Theological Seminary, Mervin Otero gave a sermon on this subject opening my eyes to the need for us to speak out when we see wrong being done, otherwise we are as guilty as the oppressor.

15. Ibid.

16. For an insightful explanation of why this is happening read, A People's History of the United States, Howard Zinn.

CHAPTER 1:

1. Howard Thurman's Jesus and the Disinherited.

2. A New Vision of Jesus, by Marc J. Borg explains the challenges by Jesus to contemporary society in his time.

3. Ibid.

4. My own experience is one of being in prison for the last 14 years.

5. Robert Mueller, in his book How, then shall we live,

shares a superior glimpse of what is important in our lives and how sometimes the tragedies of life break us open, so that we can see who we are. This is not always a pleasant experience, but it is my hope that by explaining this realization that others may come to know themselves a little better.

6. Ibid.

7. Anthony Joye shared this modem day parable in a conversation we were having about life itself. I believe this is an example of a messenger angel.

8. Peace Pilgrim's <u>Inner Peace</u> was based on these principles. My friend Adrianne first sent me a pamphlet about this courageous woman who gave up everything including her name to walk for peace.

9. In Alethia, a Community-prisoner newsletter, I wrote an article based on this.

10. As part of <u>Our Lady of Hope Catholic program</u> Father Ronald Lemmert has invited a potter named Ray Boswell to the church on several different occasions. This man recently stated that when sculpturing he lets the spirit within take control. Boswell's livelihood is making 6,000 clay creations each year as the Spirit within guides him and this newfound calling.

11. As part of my prison experience cooking has been a way of crossing cultural boundaries and nourishing the soul through this experience. <u>Prison Cuisine: A Creative Challenge</u>, an article I wrote appearing in Alethia, a community- prisoner sponsored newsletter.

12. The Walking Drum, Louis L'amour.

13. Elva Norian originally came to the Nassau County Correctional Center where I was incarcerated. She is a very spiritual woman who believes in the teachings of Jesus.

14. The full text of this article God's Way appeared in The Contributor, a Newsletter project begun by prisoners and Quakers Purchase Meeting. Copies of The Contributor are available through Hank Elkins of the Scarsdale Quaker meeting in Scarsdale, New York.

15. This article was shared with me by my friend, Adrienne Simidian, an enlightened spirit.

16. There have been a handful of these in the last century, men like Martin Luther King, Jr., Malcolm X, John F. Kennedy and many others who have died for the struggle.

17. Ishon (Winston Williams) is a man who has introduced me to the world of Meta-physics which is a blessing I deeply appreciate. He also was the one who identified my spiritual identity and I believe has coined the phrase, as he himself is a seeker.

Chapter 2:

1. I was first called a "soft soul" by a Chinese woman I had met sitting at a bar many years ago. I had never heard that term or been called as such. But as I thought about her comment, I knew she was right. Moments after this happened, I went to the men's room, and when I returned, she was gone This was at an exceptionally low ebb in my life, having just gone

through a difficult divorce Today, I view this woman as a messenger angel, for God knew what I needed even before I did. I also meet a soft soul in the county jail, Ms. Smith, who was a spiritual person first, then a guard. This is a rare occurrence.

2. Sue Glover is a member of Switzerland Yearly Meeting, and has shared the article, <u>Experimenting With Light</u>.

3. New York Theological Seminary, Sing Sing Extension program is the only master's degree program in the State prison system in New York. This unique program is privately funded. For a complete description of how this program became a reality see <u>Led By Spirit</u> written by Bill Webber and available from NYTS.

4. <u>Led By The Spirit</u>. Bill Webber gives a thorough explanation as to how New York Theological Seminary survived amid the early 70's and how today it is one of the most unique Seminaries in the world for teaching and preparing men and women for Urban Ministry. Also discussed is how the Sing Sing Master's Degree program became a reality.

5. Katherine Vockins, a volunteer and director of this program, has helped men and outside guests work with one another crossing the cultural, religious, and ethical barriers to see that of the creative essence within. I recently was in a play, <u>The Sacrifice</u>, written by a fellow prisoner, David Britton making me more aware of the spiritual communication that all people can share.

6. Victor E Frankel who spent three years in different

concentration camps in Germany wrote a book titled, <u>Man's Search for Meaning</u>. He describes how some people have the ability to rise above their circumstances and look to others who may be worse off than their own situation. In this sense, we may be able to help others and find meaning in our own life.

7. <u>Joshua</u>, Joseph Girzone

8. These principles are explained wonderfully in Thurman's book and should be read by every person who stands with "their back to the wall". IF we understood these principles this world would surely be different,

Chapter 3:

1. See: <u>This Do in Remembrance of Me</u> by Gilbert L. Johnson (Friends Journal. 1999). A new view of the Last Supper is explained in a wonderful and fresh perspective.

2. When I first read this poem the author was anonymous, today the author has come forth and told how God was talking with her in a time of difficulty in her life.

3. A quote from Lao Tse, I read in a book loaned to me by my friend Adrianne. <u>Instructions to the Cook</u>, by Bernard Glassman & Rick Fields is a wonderful guide to understand life as a specially prepared meal with insight into our connectedness in the world and our own spirituality.

Chapter 4:

1. For a professionally researched view of why this is

happening read, <u>A People's History of the United States,</u> Howard Zinn.

2. <u>The Rich Get Richer and the Poor get Prison</u>. Jeffrey Reiman gives an eye-opening portrayal of our government's prison policy.

3. <u>The Upside Down Kingdom.</u> Donald B. Kraybill is a good source of Jesus's unconventional wisdom.

4. Thurman, Ibid.

5. <u>What Prisons do to People</u>. Daniel Hellerstien- Defenders Association 1985 report.

6. <u>The Rich Get Richer and the Poor get Prison</u>. Jeffrey Reiman. A must read for anybody who really wants to know what is happening with prisons.

7. <u>Expect a Miracle</u>. Dan Wakefield presents an interesting view of common day miracles happening to ordinary people. I had the pleasure of meeting Mr. Wakefield as a guest of the NYTS program.

Chapter 5:

1. I say this because my father somehow was in tune with the creative essence within. Whether it was painting, poetry writing, cooking or even his manner of fathership he seemed to always have the right answers and they were always based in love.

2. Gustavo Gutierrez in his book, <u>On Job</u> gives us a well-reasoned definition of God's free and unmerited love,

especially to the poor and forgotten and those who lack intellectual understanding. The babes of this world Intro, xii-xiii.

Chapter 6:

1. George Fox was a mystic and also a firm believer in the existence of our ability to tap into the spiritual world. It would seem to me that this experience was a birth of the Spirit within Fox's being.

2. Invisible Man, Ralph Ellison. Although these ideas came before reading this classic book I would recommend it to every person who wants to understand a little bit better the world of invisibility and one of the greatest writers ever.

Chapter 7:

1. Jesus in the Nineteenth Century and After, Heinrich Weina & Alban G. Widgery p.405 (Jesus and the Disinherited p. 75).

2. A New Vision of Jesus, by Marc J. Borg explains the challenges by Jesus to contemporary society in his time.

3. The Upside Down Kingdom. Donald B Kraybill

4. Led By the Spirit. Bill Webber gives an exceptional story as to how New York Theological Seminary survived during the early 70's and how today it is one of the most unique Seminaries in the world for teaching and preparing men and women for Urban

Ministry.

5. Ibid.

Chapter 8:

1. <u>Space, Time and Self</u>. E Norman Pearson.

BIBLIODEX

Aquinas, St. Thomas, *75, 116*

Borg ,Marcus J, <u>A New Vision of Jesus</u>. 1998 Harper Collins Sacramento, California, *1, 108*

Buddha, *24, 73, 76,116*

Carlson. Richard, <u>Don't Sweat the Small stuff</u>. - 1997 Hyperion Publishers, New York, NY, *75*

Chambers, Oswald, <u>Power for Living</u>. May 1999 *xx*

Chapman, Mark, <u>Christianity on Trial</u>, 1996 Orbis Press, New York, NY, *47, 48, 50*

Cleage, Albert, 4*8, 49*

Confucius, *xvii*

Das, Lama Surya, <u>Awakening the Buddha Within</u>. 1997 Broadway Books, New York, NY, *23, 24*

De Chardin, Teilhard, xxi

Dev, Guru, <u>Aging with Wisdom</u>, 1998, 18, 19

Dostoyevsky, <u>Dogmatic Consitution on the Church</u>, 1964, Vatican, *29*

Ellison, Ralph, <u>Invisible Man</u>. 1994 Random House, New York, NY, 91

Ellsberg, Robert, <u>All Saints</u>, 1997 Cross Road Publishing Co., New York, NY, *10*

Fox's, George, <u>Journal of</u>, 1976, Friends United Press, Richmond, Indiana, *xix, 77, 88, 96, 111, 116*

Frankel, Victor, <u>Man' s Search for Meaning.</u> 1959 Beacon Press, Boston. Mass., *31*

Galleano, Eduardo, <u>The Book of Embraces.</u> *xv*

Gandhi, Mahatma, *xv, 10, 63, 96, 98, 116*

Garcia, Ishmael, <u>Dignidad.</u> 1997 Abingdon Press, Nashville, Tennessee, 94

Girzone, Joseph, Joshua. 1987 Macmillan Publishing Co. New York, NY (Collier Books) *2, 33, 112*

Girzone, Joseph, Joshua and the City. 1995 Doubleday Publishing, New York, *NY, 10, 50*

Glassman & Fields, Instructions to the Cook, 1996 Crown Publishers, New York, NY, *2*

Griffin, John, Black Like Me, 1982, *34*

Gutierrez, Gustavo, On Job, 1987 Orbis Books, Maryknoll, NY, *xv, xxiv, 32, 74, 110, 118*

Hammarskjold, Dag, *39*

Ireanaes, St., Bishop of Lions, *12*

Johnston, L. Gilbert, This Do in Remembrance of Me, Sept. 1999, Friends Journal, *40*

Kraybill, David, The Upside Down Kingdom , 1978 Herald Press Philadelphia, Penn., *48, 107*

L'amour, Louis, The Walking Drum. 1985 Bantam Publishers New York NY, *16*

Lazarre, Janet, Beyond the Whiteness of Whiteness. 1995 New York , NY, *67*

Lozofl: Bo, We're All Doing Time, 1987 Ashram Prison Project, California, *39*

Marshall, Calvin, *48*

May, Rollo. Love and Will, 1969 W.W. Norton Publishers, New York, *NY, xxii*

Merton, Thomas, *31*

Morrison, Toni, Beloved, 1997, *32*

Mother Janet Stuart, *11*

Grifiihs, Dom Bede, *19*

Mueller, Robert, How Then Shall we Live, 7

Muggeridge, Malcolm, Guidepost Magazine 1999 *xvi*

Peale Norman Vincent, Source of Courage, Guidepost Magazine, 1998, *20*

Pearson, Norman E., Space, Time and Self, Theosophical Publishing House, 1992, Wheaton, IL, *121*

Penn, William, *42*
Pilgrim, Peace, <u>Friends of,</u> 1983 Hemet, California, *9*
Pushon, John (Quaker), *77*
Arriens, Jan, <u>The Place of Jesus in Quaker Universalism,</u> 1990
Quaker Universalist Group, *116*
Pascal, *118*
Quaker, <u>Friends General Conference</u>, 1982 Philadelphia, PA
Rarnabai, Pandita, *124*
Reinman, Jeffrey, <u>The Rich Get Richer and the Poor Get
Prison,</u> l995 Allyn & Bacon Publishers, Boston, Mass, *48, 64*
Rivera, Angel L., <u>Releasing our Human Dignity</u>, Voices Of
1998, New York Theological Seminary, *27*

www.ingramcontent.com/pod-product-compliance
Lightning Source LLC
Chambersburg PA
CBHW060538130626
46553CB00002B/812